W9-DGG-536

RUBENSTEIN & RYNECKI, ESQS
Attorneys at Law
16 Court Street, Suite 1717
Tel: 718-522-1020 • Toll Free (800) 447-HURT
RubRynLaw@AOL.com

We are pleased to present you with a complementary copy of our book "The Outrageous Rubenstein", How a Media Savvy Trial Lawyer Fights for Justice and Change, by Sanford Rubenstein. We hope you enjoy reading it.

In the future, if we can be of assistance to you, a member of your family, or any friends, please feel free to call us at any time for a free consultation.

SANFORD RUBENSTEIN
SCOTT RYNECKI

THE OUTRAGEOUS RUBENSTEIN

THE OUTRAGEOUS RUBENSTEIN

How a Media-Savvy Trial Lawyer
Fights for Justice and Change

SANFORD RUBENSTEIN, ESQ.
with
ROYCE FLIPPIN

Foreword by Reverend Al Sharpton

Cover and book design by Susan Welt Design

Library of Congress Control Number: 2009910882

ISBN: 978-0-615-30837-1

10 9 8 7 6 5 4 3 2 1

Printed in China
through Four Colour Print Group,
Louisville, Kentucky

To my young grandsons Myles and Marcus:
May you grow up in a better world
than the one we live in now.

CONTENTS

———

Foreword by Reverend Al Sharpton   *ix*

Preface   *1*

Chapter One: FIGHTING FOR CHANGE   9

Chapter Two: MAKING DRUNK DRIVERS PAY   *17*

Chapter Three: TORTURE IN THE PRECINCT HOUSE   *27*

Chapter Four: BOMBS OVER VIEQUES   *73*

Chapter Five: JUSTICE FOR ZONGO!   99

Epilogue: THE FIGHT CONTINUES   *153*

Permissions   *165*

Index   *167*

To me, the core purpose of American democracy is to guarantee equal protection under the law and equal opportunity. When either of those threads in society unravel, America can neither live up to its promise nor approach its dreams. There have been times in American history when these American ideals have collided with American reality, forcing us as a nation to confront our shortcomings. The civil rights movement, the women's suffrage movement, the right to unionize movement, the fight for gay and lesbian rights, and any number of other movements all came into being because of a feeling that some people were being treated differently when it came to equal protection under the law. At those times, there were certain Americans who would stand in the gap at great risk, and sometimes with great unpopularity, to call for the bridging of that gap. These irritants would stay there until there was progress and until there was justice.

Usually these people, by the nature of their mission, are other than ordinary—even extraordinary. Because, as Martin Luther King, Jr. used to say, ordinary people don't challenge the system. It takes people who are other than ordinary to take the risk and to step outside their comfort zone in order to force society to stop doing what too many of us quietly allow. One such irritant—one such American—is the Outrageous Rubenstein.

I first met Sanford Rubenstein when we both became involved in the Abner Louima police brutality case in New York. Abner, a Haitian immigrant who had been sodomized and tortured by police in a Brooklyn station house, had become a symbol of a long-standing fight against police misconduct, a fight that has included such other high-profile cases as the beating of Rodney King in Los Angeles and the shooting death of Amadou Diallo in New York. For years, I've been at the forefront of the fight to uphold the idea that police must operate under the law and not above the law. This struggle has often made us targets of police unions and police-friendly media, who have tried to distort our quest by portraying us as being anti-police, rather than anti-police brutality.

Needless to say, although tens of thousand have marched and even gone to jail with us, those who had established themselves economically and socially in society usually didn't want to risk their stature and their comfort by fighting the police unions. After I'd met with Abner and helped bring his plight to the nation's attention, I remember getting a call from a local Congressman telling me that one of Abner's attorneys would be Sanford Rubenstein, who had done some work for the Louima family. The family knew I would be appearing that night on national television with Larry King, the Congressman said, and would appreciate it if I spoke kindly of Attorney Rubenstein, because there were certain other attorneys attached to the case who did not want to respect the family's choice to involve him.

That night, when Larry King said something that opened up the subject, I fulfilled my commitment to the Congressman and the Louima family and commended Brother Rubenstein, whom I had not met, but who I was assured was a fellow soldier in the struggle for justice.

The next day, tens of thousands of people began gathering in Prospect Park for a march across the Brooklyn Bridge to protest what had happened to Abner. As I arrived and walked under the arch in the plaza to what would be the front line of the march, a short, flamboyantly dressed white gentleman walked over to me with a broad smile and said, "I'd like to introduce myself, Reverend Al—I'm Brother Rubenstein!"

That began a friendship and alliance and bond that has stretched over the past decade. Sandy has been with me through many cases and investigations. He has been the object of media attacks and media praise. He visited with me in the Federal jail in Puerto Rico and then, after I was transferred to Brooklyn, spent virtually every day with me as I served the remainder of my 90-day sentence for protesting the Navy's use of Vieques as a bombing range. He has been at my side when heads of state have come to address my gatherings in New York City as well as when I journeyed to meet with them in their own countries. He has been with me in inner-city basements talking to victims' families and traveled with me to meet with the survivors of modern day slavery in Sudan. He's joined me at conferences with the heads of government in Israel and at an unforgettable lunch with Yassir Arafat, where I listened, amazed, as he and Arafat discussed the effects of garlic on male virility—this, while a hundred reporters were waiting downstairs to hear the results of Arafat's and my discussion of

Middle East policy!

That's the Outrageous Rubenstein: always on the cutting edge, always rolling with the punches, always willing to stand up—knowing that, with his flamboyant attire and quotable tongue, he would also stand out.

I guess what's most striking to me is the fact that Sandy didn't have to stand up. When I met him, he was economically secure and part of a social set, with homes in the Hamptons and South Beach as well as an amazing penthouse on New York's Upper East Side. He certainly wasn't going to profit financially from his involvement in our movement, and he certainly wasn't going to be applauded by those in his social circle. He would even be suspected by people within the movement as to what was his motives were and what was he really up to. But no matter what the attack—from either side, friend or foe—and no matter how cantankerous the victim or unappreciative the victor, Sandy hung in there. And through the test of time, one came to know that he truly believed in the basic, fundamental pursuit of justice.

I guess it all came together for me, this marriage of sincerity and outrageousness, when, on a hot summer day in 2003, Sandy was part of a delegation I led to Ghana, seeking peace talks with warring factions from Liberia who were meeting there. As we stood in Ghana's onetime slave camps with noted scholar Dr. Cornel West, Dr. Martin Luther King's former aide Reverend Al Sampson and others, listening to our guide tell us the horror stories of slavery—how hundreds had to crowd into these dark caves that could only comfortably seat fifty, and how they would have to stand there and urinate on themselves, waiting to go through the door of no return that would either bring them across the Atlantic to slavery or see them die in the midst of the voyage—Sandy began crying, as we all did, and talked about the sojourn of his people, and their need for justice, and how in that dark cave he thought of his parents, who had passed away, and the sense of justice they had instilled in him. It was there that we all realized we were fellow journeymen on the same journey of justice.

As a Brooklynite growing up, I knew that people who got on the train at different stops would sometimes be headed to the same place. Sandy didn't get on at my stop, but I've always been convinced that we are headed to the same location. It's been a ride that has sometimes been easy and sometimes been bumpy. A ride through dark tunnels and bright stations. A ride with interesting characters that get on and get off. But so far we've stayed on the train and in the same car. And I'm convinced that when we pull in, the Outrageous Rubenstein will still be on board.

Maybe it takes the outrageous to give voice to the unheard, the misunderstood, and the marginalized. And if it takes outrageousness to get us where we have to go, then I hope, as you read this book, you will unlock the outrageous part of yourself, and get on board with us.

Reverend Al Sharpton
New York City

PREFACE

THERE'S BEEN A LOT of talk lately about how civil lawsuits are hurting America. Jury awards are being blamed for everything from rising medical costs to corporate bankruptcies, and right-wing politicians are trumpeting the need for "tort reform," such as financial caps on medical malpractice lawsuits. Trial lawyers are now held up as the new villains, responsible for everything that's wrong with our nation. Even the jury system is under attack: In New York City, Mayor Michael Bloomberg has said that he wants all civil matters involving the city of New York to be decided by a judge, rather than a jury of one's peers.

You may not be surprised to learn that I take a very different view of things. Speaking as an attorney who has been involved in literally thousands of civil cases over the past 37 years, it's my strong belief that the ability of an average person to pursue a civil case—to bring a suit against an individual, a corporation or other group, or a government entity, and have his or her case heard by a jury of fellow citizens—is one of the most important rights we have as Americans. The U.S. civil justice system levels society's playing field, by giving ordinary people a means of fighting back when they've been wronged.

Think about it: Under what other system could the average man and woman on the street, often possessing little or no savings, afford to hire the very best lawyers in the country to represent them in court against large corporations or the government? This is possible because trial lawyers get paid on a contingency basis: If a civil suit is successful, the legal team typically gets one third of the final settlement. If it's not, then the client doesn't owe the lawyers a fee.

For people in our society who lack power or large financial resources, the ability to file a civil lawsuit is the only truly effective tool they have to protect themselves and their families from being taken advantage of by those who *do* have power and wealth.

Civil suits are also important for another reason, as well: They are one of the most effective ways ever devised for bringing about positive social change. It was a series of civil suits, not Federal regulation, that got rid of cancer-causing asbestos in our homes, schools and office buildings. *Brown v. Board of Education*, the landmark case that led to segregation in schools being outlawed in the United States, was a civil lawsuit as well, brought by a group of Topeka parents. Citizens' lawsuits—along with the concern that they might be brought—have also resulted in an untold number of dangerous products being pulled off the market, from the fire-prone Ford Pinto to the allegedly heart-attack-provoking medication Vioxx.

One of the most important things that we trial lawyers do is to act as a safeguard for the public against the excesses of corporate

America. Jury awards are the tool we use to hold companies accountable for unsafe products and policies—and if they're capped to the point of insignificance, this leverage will be lost. As for the charge that jury awards are driving up the cost of doing business in the U.S., I would suggest the actual cost of these awards—which are usually reduced sharply by appeals courts anyway—add up to a miniscule percentage of the nation's business expenses, and that the price tag is well worth the benefits in terms of protecting the American public.

Another favorite accusation leveled by businesses and right-wing politicians is that our civil justice system is overrun by "frivolous" lawsuits. While it may be true that some lawsuits cross over the line into silliness, these are always quickly weeded out of the system and dismissed. The overwhelming majority of civil suits that come to trial involve very serious issues, and are brought by average Americans seeking justice for themselves or a family member who was severely injured or even killed as the result of someone else's wrongful or negligent actions.

There was nothing frivolous about the case brought by a client of mine whose two children were run over and killed before her eyes, directly in front of one of Manhattan's major hospitals. As it turned out, the truck that ran them over had a blind spot as the result of inadequate side mirrors, and the city of New York had also gravely mistimed its crossing signals at that particular intersection. Carelessness and miscues had created an accident waiting to happen.

A jury heard this case, and awarded the mother $25 million in damages—at that time one of the largest jury awards in history. (Like most jury awards, it was later reduced significantly by an appellate court, to $3 million.) The jury award had a dual purpose:

Besides providing fair compensation to the victims, the monetary damages will help prevent a similar tragedy from occurring in the future by making it too expensive for truck companies not to make sure they have proper mirrors, and by sending a strong message to municipalities across America that they need to pay attention to their traffic signals—particularly the amount of time allotted for pedestrians to cross the street.

Civil suits also act as a deterrent to those individuals and organizations that cause harm to others. I'm currently participating as a member of a team of trial lawyers in a civil case in which over 3,000 victims of the September 11, 2001 terrorist attacks are suing the various individuals, organizations and financial institutions who helped bankroll the 9/11 terrorists. If the suit is successful, these groups will discover that the funding of terrorists carries a steep price tag, making it that much harder for terrorist groups to get financing in the future.

Finally, civil lawsuits are an essential tool for making sure our government is functioning correctly, and for protecting ordinary citizens against government's excesses. This is particularly true when it comes to misconduct by law-enforcement officials. It's been my experience that most police officers are good, decent people. But for certain rogue cops, the gun and the badge provide a license for careless, overly aggressive, or even sadistic behavior. Police violence against civilians remains one of the biggest problems in our country today—especially for people of color. Over the past 37 years, I've represented numerous people who were wrongly victimized by law-enforcement officers. In the process, I've learned firsthand how deeply ingrained the problem of police brutality is, and how important it is for police to be held accountable for their misconduct in both criminal and civil court.

In this book, I discuss several high-profile cases in which I've represented victims of wrongdoing. As you'll see, each of these cases brought about a different and important change in the way our system operates, and made our society fairer and safer in the process. Along the way, I'll provide a glimpse of how a major lawsuit looks from the inside. I'll share some of my experiences as a lawyer—including the hard-won lesson of how important it is to work with the media in waging the all-important "trial before the trial" in the court of public opinion—and show why it's so important to protect our civil justice system from the current attacks by big business and conservative politicians.

To expand on this last point for a moment, just imagine if the "no juries" approach favored by Mayor Bloomberg for cases involving city agencies became law. This would essentially create a two-tiered system of justice: When a person of means, who uses a private hospital, lives in a privately owned or rented apartment, and rides taxis around town is injured, that person would be free to sue and have their case heard by an impartial jury. But if a similar injury should happen to a person of lesser means while being treated at a public hospital, or living in municipal housing, or riding the public transportation system, he or she would be denied the right to a jury trial!

To me, the ability for an ordinary person to file a civil lawsuit and have his or her case heard by a jury is the only way that average citizens can stand up to government and major corporations and get redress for wrongs committed against them. As the following pages will show, it's an important right—and one worth protecting.

This book is about my life and experiences as a lawyer, and about the small part I've been able to play in the ongoing fight for equal justice for all Americans. In Chapter One, you'll read about how I became trial lawyer, starting with my early days at a storefront law practice in the tough Bedford-Stuyvesant section of Brooklyn. In Chapter Two, I describe a landmark case in which I represented a mother whose son suffered brain damage when he was struck by a drunk driver in an incident that claimed the life of his best friend. This horrible tragedy led to a significant toughening of New York State's DWI laws, thanks to a heroic lobbying effort on the part of my client and the mother of the boy who had been killed.

Chapter Three tells the story of my most famous client, Abner Louima—a fine man who had emigrated to America from Haiti searching for a better life, only to be falsely arrested and beaten by New York City police, then sodomized savagely with a stick inside a police precinct house bathroom and left to bleed nearly to death on the floor of a jail cell. The civil case we brought against the city of New York, the New York Police Department, and the Police Benevolent Association directly resulted in a major shift in police policy, by which an independent legal counsel is now provided for officers who witness acts of misconduct by their peers. Abner's case also contributed to other important changes, including the eventual elimination of the so-called "48-hour rule," which gave police officers a two-day reprieve before undergoing questioning by the NYPD's administrative investigators.

Chapter Four recounts my role in assisting Reverend Al Sharpton as he employed an act of civil disobedience to successfully bring a halt to the U.S. Navy's use of the Puerto Rican island of Vieques as a bombing site—an odyssey that included a 90-day jail term for Sharpton, during which I spent every day by his side.

Finally, Chapter Five describes the tragic case of Ousmane Zongo, an unarmed African artisan who, while going about his business, was chased down and shot dead by a plainclothes police officer in the Manhattan warehouse where he plied his trade. My efforts in representing his widow and family helped bring about significant changes in the way plainclothes officers are trained and deployed in New York City.

By shining a spotlight on unsafe corporate practices, regulatory and statutory shortcomings, and misconduct by law enforcement and other government entities—and by helping to make sure the responsible parties are held accountable for their actions, both criminally and civilly—I believe that we trial lawyers can and will make a difference, today and in the future. My hope and goal is to use the power of our civil justice system to help create a safer and more equitable society for everyone, so that my two young grandsons might grow up in a better world than the one we now live in.

A few years back, one of New York's best-known tabloids, the *New York Post*, referred to me as "the...outrageous Rubenstein" in an editorial criticizing my legal defense of my client, the Reverend Al Sharpton, in the course of a proceeding involving some monies allegedly owed by Sharpton's civil rights organization, the National Action Network. I took this editorial comment, obviously intended to be a pejorative, in quite the opposite spirit. I've made it a habit in my career to stand up against powerful institutions on behalf of ordinary citizens. While that might make my actions outrageous to some, being called "The Outrageous Rubenstein" is, to me, a compliment of the highest order.

Sanford "Sandy" Rubenstein
Brooklyn, NY

CHAPTER ONE

FIGHTING FOR CHANGE

As a trial attorney, my role really boils down to one thing: fighting for change. Tragedies often happen quickly—but they're usually the result of unsafe practices or conditions that have been allowed to develop and fester over time. Whenever I'm representing an injured party in court, seeking monetary damages or other considerations, my goal is not only to obtain a just and equitable outcome for my client, but also to do my best to help eliminate whatever dangerous behaviors or conditions allowed the injury to occur in the first place, so that similar tragedies won't happen again.

The Sean Bell case is a perfect example of this. Bell was killed in 2006, shot down in a hail of 50 police bullets after leaving a bachelor party at a strip club on the morning of his wedding day. I, along with Michael Hardy—as fine a trial lawyer as you'll find today—was asked to represent Nicole Paultre Bell, Sean Bell's fiancée and the mother of his children, and Bell's companions, Joseph

Guzman and Trent Benefield, who were seriously wounded in the same shooting.

Having worked with Hardy on the Ousmane Zongo case, which I discuss at length in Chapter Five, I was glad to be collaborating with him again. Besides being a brilliant legal strategist, he is someone who carries the cause and objectives of today's civil rights movement in his very heart and soul. Hardy has served with distinction as general counsel to the National Action Network, Reverend Al Sharpton's civil rights organization, since its formation, and he's devoted his life to keeping the movement going forward. He also has a wonderfully calm demeanor, which complements my own more aggressive nature very well—making us a great team.

The Sean Bell shooting got a huge amount of attention in the local and national media, and eventually resulted in serious criminal charges against three of the detectives involved—but the widespread outrage and attendant legal proceedings over the shooting produced one important response from the city of New York well before the detectives ever came to trial: In June, 2007, seven months after Sean's death, New York police commissioner Ray Kelly officially accepted a high-level panel's list of 19 recommended changes in the way the NYPD's undercover operations were conducted. These changes included psychological screening for all police officers who were candidates for undercover assignments, and a critically important proposal that any police officer who shoots someone be required to take a post-shooting Breathalyzer test.

This last item was a direct response to one of the biggest questions surrounding the Sean Bell case: *how much alcohol had the detectives consumed inside the strip club prior to the shooting?* NYPD guidelines allowed undercover police working in a club or

bar setting to have two alcoholic drinks during an eight-hour period—a rule that can easily be broken, especially when you're hang-
ing out in a club for hours on end. No one will ever know for sure
how many drinks each detective had actually downed on the night
Sean was killed. Frankly, the idea of *any* alcohol being consumed
on duty by officers who have been granted the special power to use
a gun is, to me, a bad idea. But at least this new rule will act as a
deterrent to undercover detectives breaking the two-drink limit,
and to police officers drinking alcohol while on duty in general—
and the public will be safer as a result. It's my hope that this new
policy ends up being a model for police departments across the
nation.

The NYPD's policy shift in the rules governing undercover police
work as a result of the Bell case is exactly the kind of social change
I've spent my legal career working to bring about—going back to
my very earliest days as an attorney in the 1970s and early '80s,
when I plied my trade at a storefront law practice in the Bedford-
Stuyvesant section of Brooklyn. The practice had been started by
Bill and Al Jacobs, two brothers who were then in their sixties. For
most of his adult life Bill had commercial interests in Brooklyn that
included owning a liquor store across the street from our law office,
where for years he'd practiced law on the side, representing people
in the neighborhood. Meanwhile, his brother Al had risen to the
rank of police captain with the NYPD, retiring as a deputy inspec-
tor. When they stepped down from their respective careers, they
decided to start a small law practice at a storefront opposite the
liquor store, in what had formerly been a print shop.

By the time I began working there—first as a law clerk, during
my last year in law school, and then as a partner after I'd graduated

from law school and been admitted to the bar—the storefront had mushroomed into a thriving practice. It was a tough neighborhood, and our clients were mainly bodegas, liquor stores, victims of personal injury, and some local individuals who had been accused of crimes. I got thrown into the arena right away: The day I was sworn in to the New York State bar, I had to skip a celebration lunch with my father to begin the jury selection for my first trial, in which I was defending a man indicted for the felony of buying heroin. On the morning I was scheduled to address the jury with my summation, I was so nervous, knowing a man's freedom was at stake, that I actually threw up before leaving home. When the jury voted for an acquittal, the only person more surprised than me was my client!

My first really high-profile case occurred in 1976, when I was asked to defend a young woman accused of shoplifting a sweater from E.J. Korvette's, the now-defunct discount department store. A recent arrival from mainland China, she had gained her freedom six months earlier by swimming through open water from Chinese territory to Hong Kong. Sitting in my office with her cousin along to interpret, the woman told me what had actually taken place at Korvette's: She had walked into the store carrying a bag containing a sweater that she'd purchased earlier at another store. After buying a second sweater at Korvette's, she was about to leave the store when she was stopped by a security guard who took her to an empty room and proceeded to sexually molest her. Eventually, the guard realized he was mistaken about the sweater and asked her to sign a waiver promising not to bring any civil action against the store. She refused to sign, at which point the store's chief of security and two other guards were summoned. When she still wouldn't sign the document, the chief began hitting her, cutting her mouth and bruising her body. She continued to stand fast, so the security staff called the police and had her arrested for shoplifting.

She ended up spending the night in jail, and was clearly still upset when I met with her. But she was also determined to set the record straight and clear her name. Personally, I was appalled at such a blatant miscarriage of justice. I immediately got in touch with the Brooklyn District Attorney's office and ultimately was able to persuade them to open an investigation. A city detective was sent to the store, where he asked to see the bag containing the allegedly shoplifted sweater. When he unsealed the bag, it was empty. The security employee told him to wait a minute—then came back with a resealed bag containing a different sweater than the one that was supposedly stolen!

At that point, the jig was up. One of the four guards involved was offered immunity by prosecutors and he confessed to everything. The other three employees were charged with assault, conspiracy and perjury. Meanwhile, all criminal charges against my client were dropped.

When the story about the arrests of the security guards broke, it made a big splash in the New York media. I got a call from the district attorney's people, asking me to come by their offices the next day. When I arrived there, to my surprise, I was immediately ushered into a conference room jammed with reporters and cameras. It was my first exposure to a high-profile press conference. Before things started rolling, the district attorney pulled me aside. "I want you to just sit there, and leave everything to me," he said. I did as he asked, sitting meekly in my chair while he held court for the press. Today, having had the leading role myself in countless press conferences, I look back on that moment and have to laugh. I doubt any prosecutor would make that request now!

One thing hasn't changed, though: Even in those early days, I had an instinct for saying the right thing. When my local paper in Rockland County, where I was living at the time, interviewed me about the case, I explained everything that had happened to my client—including the fact that she'd ended up seeking psychiatric treatment afterwards—and concluded by telling the reporter, "No human being should have to go through this." Re-reading that article today, several decades later, as a veteran of numerous press conferences, my comment still sounds on target and very appropriate to me.

With my client's criminal charges now disposed of, I went on to file a $7 million civil suit on her behalf against Korvette's. The suit was eventually settled out of court for a fair amount of money damages. This case taught me the value of a determined, honest prosecutor, and also gave me a renewed respect for how the justice system can serve as a tool for defending the powerless.

Around that same time, I had two other fairly high-profile cases that somewhat dampened my enthusiasm for criminal defense work. In one of the cases, I defended a man accused in the rape of a frail, elderly woman. The other case, which made the front page of the *New York Daily News*, involved a white Jewish boy who had been killed the night before his wedding. I was defending the accused killer. Before the trial started, the judge presiding over the case took me aside and explained the deal being offered to my client by the prosecutors: My client would get 15 years if he copped a plea of guilty, and most likely 25 years to life if he pleaded innocent and was convicted.

I took my client to the back of the courtroom and outlined the proposed deal to him. "I'm a young man," my client replied. "I can do up to 15 years, and if I cop to the charge I'll probably get out sooner. But I can't do 25—I'd have spent so much time in prison by that time, I'm afraid I wouldn't be able to function on the outside. Tell him I'll take the offer."

I informed the judge that we were accepting the plea bargain.

At that point I knew that my days as a criminal defense lawyer were numbered. I had started trying civil cases by then, and was doing very well at it—sometimes even "ringing the bell," a trial lawyer's term for convincing a jury to give the maximum possible award in a court of lower jurisdiction, which at that time was $10,000. I was also discovering that I felt a greater sense of accomplishment from trying civil cases. I particularly liked the fact that civil suits were generally about standing up for the little guy who had been wronged, and who often had no one else to turn to.

While our Bedford-Stuyvesant storefront law office was a good place for a young attorney starting out in his career, it could also be dangerous. One day in the mid-1980s, I was sitting at my desk going over some paperwork when two men walked in, one of them gripping the other in a headlock with a gun pointed to his head. The man in the headlock was a regular client of our law office, a neighborhood numbers runner who frequently needed legal representation and was in and out of the office constantly. Keeping his hold on my client, the other fellow swung his gun around and trained it on me. Since I was on good terms with my client, I assumed they were just horsing around, trying to get a rise out of me.

"Can't you see I'm working?" I said. "I don't have time for this."

That's when the guy with the gun shouted, *"Motherfucker, get up and give...me...your wallet—NOW!"* and pressed the end of the gun barrel against my temple.

I knew then he wasn't kidding, and my annoyance instantly

turned into real fear. It's a feeling you can't ever truly know until you've stared down the barrel of a gun. I handed over my wallet without a word and he left, with my client still in tow.

Thinking the incident was just a fluke, I never told my family or friends what had happened. But then, a few months later, two other men came into the storefront brandishing guns. I happened to be on the phone talking with Gary Pillersdorf, one of my best friends from law school who went on to become one of New York's finest trial lawyers, when one of the guys walked into my office, stuck out his gun and yelled, "Hands up!" I immediately dropped the phone and held my arms as high in the air as I could get them. The men herded me and several other employees of our law firm into the bathroom while robbing us of our wallets and jewelry. The whole time, we just stood there in fear, expecting shots to ring out at any moment—aimed at us. Fortunately, the men took off without firing their guns.

Pillersdorf, who was still on the open phone line, heard everything that was happening and called the police, who arrived shortly after the thieves had fled. As I joined the cops in their patrol car to search the neighborhood for the two men (unsuccessfully, as it turned out), my fear-induced adrenaline buzz quickly turned into a rush of excitement. Still, it wasn't an adventure I planned to repeat. Not long after that, I moved our offices to their present location on Court Street in the heart of downtown Brooklyn, within walking distance of all the major Brooklyn courthouses. There's plenty of action in my office these days—but thankfully, none of it involves gunplay.

CHAPTER TWO

MAKING DRUNK DRIVERS PAY

O NE OF THE MOST important aspects of fighting for change through the civil justice system is what happens *outside* the courtroom. Part of my responsibility as a lawyer is always to be involved in the media's coverage of any case involving a client of mine. This is especially important in the days and weeks immediately following whatever incident has occurred—in what I call "the trial before the trial" in the court of public opinion.

What it boils down to is this: Whenever an incident takes place that could potentially result in a criminal and/or civil trial, the media's coverage of that incident *invariably has a profound and pervasive effect on the public's perception of what happened.* And it's this same public that will ultimately make up the jury pool that provides the jurors who will decide the fate of my client's case.

'But Sandy,' I can hear you saying, 'it's not supposed to be that way!' I know, I know—every case is supposed to be brought to trial (or not) strictly on its merits, and every sitting jury is supposed to be made up of people who have absolutely no preconceived opinions about the case they're hearing. Still, the inescapable truth is that public perception has its way of influencing a jury pool, in both subtle and not-so-subtle ways.

Any lawyer who has handled high-profile cases is well aware of this fact—which is why, if you pay careful attention to the news stories in the days immediately following a high-profile incident, you'll often see a variety of details about the case being leaked to the press by different unnamed sources. Sometimes these supposed facts turn out to be completely untrue, but corrections have a hard time taking hold once something false has been implanted in the public's consciousness. I don't approve of this practice of leaking misleading information, but it happens—which is why I'm a firm believer in getting the favorable truth about your client and the accurate facts of the case out to the public as quickly as possible.

Working to get favorable coverage for my clients in the media isn't just about positioning for a future trial or settlement negotiations, though. Publicity is also an important lever in forcing changes in institutions, whether this means getting the NYPD to change its policies, pushing for new legislation on a state or Federal level, or simply keeping the pressure on to enforce existing laws, including both civil and criminal statutes. In fact, making sure that people are held legally responsible for negligent and other wrongful behavior is one of the most important aspects of making our society safer—which is why I often find myself cooperating with prosecutors.

A good example of this is the infamous Staten Island Ferry crash of 2003, which claimed 11 lives and seriously injured dozens more after the ferry pilot passed out at the controls, allowing the ferry to crash into a concrete piling at full cruising speed. As one of the lead attorneys representing victims and their families in their civil lawsuits against the city of New York, I worked actively to publicize the facts of the case. However, the most important outcome of the tragedy took place not in the civil, but in the criminal term of Federal district court, when the city's director of ferry operations pled guilty to one count of seaman's manslaughter and was sentenced to a year and a day in prison for his failure to enforce the "two-pilot rule," which requires two pilots to be in the pilothouse when the ferry is docking. If that rule had been enforced properly, the pilot who passed out would have immediately been replaced at the controls by another pilot. Instead, he was alone in the pilothouse when he became incapacitated.

As one investigative report concluded, the situation resulting from this lax enforcement was "an accident waiting to happen." The fact that the official in charge of enforcing the rules pled guilty and was sent to prison, even though he was miles from the ferry when the crash occurred, sent an extremely important message to transportation officials across the nation: If you fail to enforce the safety rules in the transit system you're overseeing, *you can go to jail.* There's no question in my mind that our nation's buses, trains, ferries and planes will be safer as a result of that criminal prosecution.

In a similar vein, one of my most satisfying moments as an attorney occurred a few years ago when the New York State legislature passed and the governor signed a criminal statute that I'd pushed very hard for. The bill, called "Vasean's Law," makes it a serious criminal felony if a person kills or injures someone else as the result of driving a car while legally intoxicated.

The bill was a bittersweet victory, for it had been inspired by the death in 2004 of 11-year-old Vasean Alleyne who, with his friend, 12-year-old Angel Reyes, was struck by a van while crossing a street in Queens. Vasean was killed almost immediately, while Angel suffered brain damage as a result of the collision. According to newspaper accounts, the driver of the van, a boiler repairman named John Wirta, had admitted to drinking beer with friends before climbing into his vehicle to drive home, and a breathalyzer test taken immediately after the incident showed that Wirta had a blood alcohol level of .13 mg/deciliter—well above New York's legal limit of .08.

The boys were struck down on Friday, October 22. The following afternoon, I picked up a message from my answering service informing me that Diana Reyes, Angel's mother, was trying to reach me. I called her back and arranged to meet her at Cornell Weill Medical Center, where Angel was lying in a coma with a brain injury, still unaware that his best friend had been killed.

As I sat with Diana Reyes in a small conference room overlooking the East River, hearing the details of the case for the first time—how two best friends, one Hispanic, one African-American, had been mowed down by a drunk driver while crossing the street, leaving one dead and the other in a coma—it immediately struck me that this was an important case that the public should be aware of. One of the most shocking aspects of the case, as I quickly discovered, was that because of the way the DWI laws in New York State were written at that time, the driver would most likely only be charged with the misdemeanor crime of driving while intoxicated—a violation that carried a maximum of one year in jail.

Needless to say, Diana and Vasean's mother, Monique Dixon, were outraged by this. In addition to filing a lawsuit for damages on behalf of her son, Angel Reyes, Diana agreed, along with Monique and me, that we would use this case as a rallying point for the passage of new, tougher DWI legislation. Under New York State law at that time, in order to charge a drunk driver with vehicular manslaughter, prosecutors had to show that he had committed some other driving violation, such as running a red light, in addition to being legally drunk. We wanted to see legislation passed that raised driving while intoxicated to a serious felony in cases where it causes death or serious injury, whether or not there was some other driving violation committed as well.

As always, the first step was to make sure the media was aware of the story, and had full access to all the facts and principals in the case. Sensing the chance to turn this already high-profile tragedy into an impetus for change, I quickly came up with a plan and ran it by my client, Diana Reyes, to get her consent. Next, I called up a reporter I knew at the *New York Daily News.* "If you and a photographer meet me at the hospital," I told him, "I can get you an interview with the mother of Angel Reyes at his bedside."

Of course, hospital rooms are supposed to be off-limits to the press—but I knew that if we kept a low profile, no one would stop us from conducting this interview and photo opportunity. Sure enough, the photographer, the reporter and I were able to walk nonchalantly off the elevator and straight into the room where Angel lay in a coma, breathing through a ventilator, as his mother sat watching over him. The photographer started snapping away at the boy and his mom. The next, day, a photo of the anxious mother and the comatose boy in his hospital bed was published up front in the Sunday *Daily News,* insuring that the story of this tragedy would be stuck forever in the minds of newspaper readers throughout the metropolitan area. The dramatic photos and accompanying story also served to fuel the general coverage of the story in the weeks that followed.

That same day, the *New York Post* ran a story about the case under the headline "Insane Law Lets Fiends Off With a Ticket and Fine." The article focused on how prosecutors were hamstrung by the shortcomings of New York's drunk-driving laws. It quoted Monique Dixon as saying, "My 11-year-old son is dead right now because somebody got behind the wheel and drank…and in the city that we live in, the law says that he is not a murderer."

The media continued to follow the story closely, providing regular reports on the recovery of Angel, who finally came out of his coma six days after being hit. It wasn't until his release from the hospital a month later, however, that he was told his best friend Vasean had been killed. It was a revelation that we handled with extreme care, after consulting with mental health experts about the best way to proceed—but he was still devastated by the news.

Meanwhile, the prosecutors had been talking to a number of people who'd witnessed the tragedy, looking for evidence of an additional driving violation by Wirta that would allow them to charge him with vehicular manslaughter. Their search turned out to be in vain: Although, according to news reports, people claimed to have seen Wirta driving erratically down the road, he hadn't run any red lights, hadn't crossed the center line, and wasn't speeding—leaving no basis for a reckless driving charge.

Wirta eventually agreed to plead guilty to driving while intoxicated in exchange for a 60-day sentence (of which he ultimately served just 38 days). His court appearances along the way included some dramatic encounters with Vasean's mother. The New York media reported that at his first appearance, in early November, Monique exploded in rage at Wirta, screaming, "Look at me, look at me!" She went on to shout, "You made a choice to drink. Do you see what your choice has done to my family?"

At another court hearing, in late Decer.
ported that Monique was waiting for Wirta wh,
the courthouse. "How does it feel to kill an inn
screamed at him. "How do you live with yourseli
was truly tragic, and the media captured it in full.

In the meantime, all this publicity made the sta.   .cal
leaders much more receptive than they might have otherwise been
to the idea of putting new, tougher drunk-driving legislation on
the books. We found out that a stiffer law had already been kick-
ing around the state capital for some time, but had gotten stuck in
Albany gridlock. It was clear to me that we had to go straight to the
highest levels of state leadership—then-Governor George Pataki,
and the state's ranking Democrat, the Speaker of the New York
State Assembly, Sheldon Silver.

In mid-November, Monique and Diana presented Silver, with
60,000 signatures on petitions and letters they'd gathered, all asking for a change in the law. Meanwhile, I was working with Tracy
Brown (daughter of the late Secretary of Commerce Ron Brown),
who was the attorney from Johnnie Cochran's law firm representing Vasean's mother, Monique Dixon, with regard to the wrongful
death of her son, in an effort to set up meetings with both men.
The meeting with Pataki took place in a conference room just outside his office in Albany. In addition to the governor, the meeting
was attended by Monique Dixon, her lawyer, Tracy Brown, Diana
Reyes, the governor's counsel, and myself. Pataki first expressed
his sympathies to the two mothers, then went on to say that he was
absolutely determined to break the gridlock and do whatever he
could to get a new bill passed and signed into law.

"Governor," I said to him, "When you sign that bill, the young
man I represent would like to have one of those pens."

"I'll make sure he gets it," Pataki said. "I'm committed to seeing this happen."

Our next visit was to the New York City offices of Sheldon Silver. He knew me, and had some kind words to say about me to Angel's mother. "I'm in total agreement that the state's DWI law need to be toughened," he told us, "and I'm committed to working to that end."

I'd told the media that we would be holding a press conference after the meeting, and a number of newspaper and TV reporters had gathered in front of the building. Once we'd all shaken hands on our shared goal of getting Vasean's Law through the state legislature, Silver's staff invited the reporters up to his conference room, where we all stood together to field their questions.

Monique was convinced, however, that even the backing of Silver, the most powerful person in the State Assembly, would not be enough to get a bill onto the governor's desk. She was absolutely right: The State Senate went on to pass a piece of legislation that included consecutive sentences in cases where drunk drivers claimed multiple victims. But as the winter wore on, the bill stalled once again in the State Assembly, where legislators were holding out for another version of the bill—one that didn't call for consecutive sentences, among other differences.

In an attempt to break the deadlock, Monique and Diana began a six-week stretch of personal lobbying, driving up to Albany and sitting down one-on-one with all 150 members of the State Assembly as well as various other lawmakers, in an attempt to persuade them to find a workable compromise. Their remarkable effort finally paid off in early May, when Pataki, Silver, and State Senate leader Joseph Bruno announced they'd reached a compromise and had a bill ready for passage by both houses, which would then be signed by the governor. "The law will make it easier for prosecutors to bring felony charges against drunken drivers who kill people in crashes; drivers convicted of vehicular manslaughter face up to seven years in prison," noted the *New York Times,* adding: "The catalyst for the passage of the law, the three leaders said, was the emotional lobbying of Monique Dixon."

A month later, Governor Pataki completed the process of making the bill a reality, signing "Vasean's Law" at a very moving ceremony inside a packed gym at P.S. 165 in Flushing, Queens, the school Vasean Alleyne had graduated from before he was killed. I attended with Angel and Diana Reyes and Monique Dixon. We gathered behind Pataki to watch as the governor put his signature to the bill, using one ceremonial pen to sign his first name and another to sign his second. Then, true to his word, he handed one of the pens to Angel and the other to Monique, Vasean's mother,

I was thrilled that an idea I had come up with while sitting with both mothers in a Queens diner—namely, to push for a law that provided tougher penalties for drunken drivers who cause a death or serious injury—had finally come about, thanks to the relentless pursuit of that goal by these two mothers.

Once the bill was signed, Monique Dixon went to the podium to address the assembly. "God chose my son to be a catalyst to save others' lives," Monique Dixon told the hushed crowd. "Today is a great day for the people of the state of New York."

A few weeks later, John Wirta entered his guilty plea in exchange for a 60-day jail sentence. Not long afterwards, working through the services of a mediator, we settled the lawsuit on behalf of Angel Reyes against Wirta and his employer (who owned the vehicle Wirta had been driving that day) for a multi-million-dollar sum.

Today, Angel—who will always have a shunt inside his head as a result of being struck by Wirta's van that October evening—is doing as well as can be expected, trying very hard to live as normal a life as he did before the tragedy. Of course, we'll never know what the full impact was on him of losing his best friend. The monetary award will help make sure Angel keeps his footing on the road to adulthood. But what will be even more important to him, I believe, is his knowledge that some positive change did result from the awful tragedy that befell him and his best friend, Vasean—and that he was a part of making it happen.

CHAPTER THREE

TORTURE IN THE PRECINCT HOUSE

"Kimbala!"

BIG THINGS OFTEN BEGIN in small ways: It was a Tuesday morning in early August, 1997, and we had just moved our law firm into a new, larger suite of offices at 16 Court Street in Brooklyn—where we were still surrounded by bare walls and minimal furniture—when one of my staff came in to tell me that she'd received a call about a man who'd been sodomized with a stick in a police station by a police officer. The caller was a prior client of mine, a Haitian-born man named Sam Nicolas. He was hoping I would represent the alleged victim, who was a cousin of his.

The whole story seemed rather unbelievable to me. Still, I always make a point of following up any request for representation. You never know—we've gotten some outlandish calls over the years that have turned into serious cases. So I sent one of our young lawyers to meet with the victim, Abner Louima, in the Brooklyn hospital where he was being treated. Before long, the lawyer was back.

He'd been unable to meet with the victim, he told me, because two criminal lawyers who were there at Louima's bedside had sent him away, telling him they'd call our firm if they needed us.

I didn't give the matter another thought until the following morning, when I saw, splashed across the front page of the *New York Daily News*, a photo of Louima sitting in his hospital bed under the banner headline: "TORTURED BY COPS."

I immediately put two and two together. "So *that's* what the call was about!" I thought. There was nothing I could do for the moment, however, except keep the two criminal lawyers' words stored away in my mental file: We'll call you if we need you.

A few days later, I got a second call from Sam Nicolas, asking me to come to a meeting at the church of his father, Pastor Philius Nicolas, the head of a large Haitian congregation in Brooklyn. Apparently Pastor Nicolas, who is also Abner Louima's uncle, wanted to talk to me about representing Louima in a civil case against the City of New York.

By this point, the story had become front-page news across the nation. Since I wasn't sure how to get to the church, I asked a well-known member of the Haitian community, Dr. Jean Claude Compas, whom I'd known for years, to come along with me in my car. We pulled up in front of the church and the two of us walked in through the lobby to the pastor's office. Mayor Giuliani had already been there and left, and there was still a heavy media and police presence outside the church. Pastor Nicolas and his son were both there, along with other community leaders. So were the two lawyers who had been at the hospital, Carl Thomas and Brian Figeroux, both of who hailed from Trinidad and Tobago in the Caribbean.

When my turn came to speak, I told the group about my

background, including the fact that I'd traveled to Haiti many times and was widely respected in New York's Haitian community. I also mentioned that I'd represented another Haitian, Jacques Camile, when he was shot by a New York City police officer several years before, and had obtained a seven-figure settlement for him from the city of New York, the NYPD, and the officer who shot him. We agreed that they would be back in touch with me after talking things over with Louima and his family.

As I was getting ready to leave, however, Thomas and Figeroux suddenly erupted. "You obsequious piece of shit!" yelled Thomas. "Bloodsucker! You're just pimping off the black community!"

Clearly, they had no conception of who I was, or my history as an activist for the Haitian community. In fact, a number of years back it had been *my* idea to float Haitian bonds as a way of boosting the impoverished island nation's economy—an idea that I'd passed along to then-President Aristide, and which he'd ended up supporting. In addition, I had been one of the leaders of a massive demonstration for democracy in Haiti after Aristide was removed from power by a coup.

"I'm Rubenstein," I told them. "The Haitians know me. They *respect* me."

None of this registered, however. With Thomas still in my face, I retreated out of the office and headed out the front door of the building, trying to get to my car, which was parked nearby. Thomas followed closely, haranguing me every step of the way. It was the longest 75 feet in my life. All I could think was, "I can't believe this is happening to me." Obviously these guys didn't want me on the case and were trying to scare me off. Having grown up in the projects, though, I don't scare easily. As the car door closed, what I was feeling wasn't fear but rather a sense of disbelief.

A couple of days later, I got a phone call from Pastor Nicolas. "Abner's expecting you at the hospital," he said. "He wants you to be his lawyer." Louima, after doing his homework and learning of my reputation in the community, had decided to override the objections of Thomas and Figeroux and hire me anyway.

Once at Brooklyn Hospital, where Louima had been transferred from Coney Island Hospital, I had to check in with two police officers stationed in the hall of the intensive care unit. The officers, members of a special unit that normally guards dignitaries, had been dispatched to the hospital by Mayor Giuliani. According to Louima, Justin Volpe—the officer accused of actually sodomizing him—had warned him that if Abner told anyone what had happened to him, Volpe would kill him and his family. With the media firestorm surrounding this case, Giuliani was taking no chances.

The two officers checked their list of approved visitors, then escorted me upstairs to the intensive care unit. When I walked into Louima's hospital room, my first thought was that he looked like he'd walked into a brick wall. Abner's face and lips were badly swollen from the beating he'd received prior to his being attacked with the stick. Lying propped up in bed, attached to various pieces of medical equipment, it was clear that he'd been through hell. The second thing that struck me immediately was how remarkably composed Abner was. Although he was in obvious pain, I was deeply impressed by his inner calm.

He'd been expecting me, and as I sat at his bedside he ran through a narrative of what had happened to him. On the night in question, after completing his shift as a night watchman, he had gone out to hear a Haitian band, the Phantoms, at a local Brooklyn nightclub. When the show finished around 4 A.M., a scuffle broke out on the sidewalk outside the club and police were called to the scene. Someone in the crowd struck one of the officers and another officer then mistakenly identified Louima as the culprit, handcuffing him and putting him into a squad car. On the way to the 70th precinct station house, Abner described how he had been beaten twice. When they finally reached the station house at around 5 A.M., according to Louima, one of the officers led him into the bathroom, where another officer joined them. As one policeman held him down, the other rammed a stick up Louima's rectum, causing severe internal injuries. Abner was then taken to a holding cell where he lay in intense pain, bleeding profusely. Eventually the police called for an ambulance, which arrived at 6:30. Following an inexplicable delay of an hour and half—as a review of the police log would later reveal—the ambulance finally left the precinct house around 8:00, taking Abner to Coney Island Hospital.

After he was done relating his horrific tale, Louima signed the necessary legal documents confirming that he was retaining my law firm. I was glad to be representing him, but I knew there would be a fierce battle ahead.

We arranged to meet again the following day. Then, at Louima's request, I drove straight from the hospital to the home of his father, where Abner's wife, Micheline, was waiting to sign the appropriate forms allowing my firm to represent Abner and herself. We were joined there by my law partner, Scott Rynecki. As always, having Rynecki by my side gave me an extra measure of confidence. Not only is he a tenacious litigator and respected negotiator, but he also brings a variety of other skills to the table. I'm lucky to have him as a colleague—both in his role of running the day-to-day operations of our law office, and also as an indispensable partner in dealing with the uncertainties that inevitably rear their head in high-profile cases like this one.

I continued to meet daily with Louima in his hospital room. During this period, he made it clear that his first priority was to get his health and strength back. One of his first requests was that I help get his young daughter, Samantha, into the United States. The offspring of a previous relationship, she was living in Haiti with her mother, who had agreed that she could come to live with Louima in New York. The paperwork for her immigration had been approved before the torture incident occurred, but her admission to the U.S. had been repeatedly delayed by bureaucratic snags. I immediately phoned the office of my good friend Congressman Edolphus "Ed" Towns, who represents Brooklyn's 10th district in Congress. He promised he would get right on the case and start cutting through the red tape.

Meanwhile, Thomas and Figeroux were still part of Louima's team as well, which inevitably led to some tense moments. Shortly after Louima had hired me, Figeroux made a not-so-veiled threat, telling me he "didn't know what the radicals will do" when they found out I was involved.

I told him, "Well you have my card—they know where to find me." Outwardly I put on a brave and nonchalant front, but inwardly I was concerned. I really didn't know what to expect.

A short time after this, while Louima was still hospitalized, he asked the three of us to meet him there. "I want you to work together," he instructed us. A few minutes later, standing in the hospital corridor outside Louima's room, I turned and offered to shake hands with Figueroux, hoping to bury the hatchet once and for all. Figeroux refused point blank. "Just because I have to work with you doesn't mean I have to shake your hand," he said, glaring at me.

As unpleasant as these encounters were, I didn't let this sort of thing bother me. My main concern was to keep public attention focused on what had happened to my client. The Haitian-American Alliance had decided to hold a large march and rally to demand justice for Louima, and they invited me to join in the discussion about who should be invited to the rally. Different names were brought up, including that of Reverend Al Sharpton. I'd never met Sharpton; all I really knew about him was what I'd learned from the media, which had generally portrayed him as a controversial figure—maybe too controversial, to my thinking. I was worried that if Sharpton got involved in the rally, *he* would become the issue, and the assault on Louima would be forgotten in the resulting media uproar.

I couldn't have been more wrong. The involvement of Sharpton and his civil rights organization, The National Action Network, ended up benefiting the march and the cause of obtaining justice for Louima immensely. In addition, I would go on to become both Sharpton's friend and his personal lawyer. Luckily, the organizers of the protest overruled me and voted to extend an invitation to the man I would come to know as "Rev."

As it turned out, Sharpton must have known something about my reputation among New York's Haitian community. A couple of days before the protest march in support of Louima, I got an excited call from Paul Jacobs, a well-respected lawyer with the firm of Fulbright Jaworski. Paul is my personal lawyer and the son of Bill Jacobs, who was one of my partners for the first 12 years of my career until he retired.

"Did you see the Larry King Show last night?" he asked.

"No. Why?"

"Reverend Al Sharpton was on the show," Paul said. "Larry King was baiting him to go after the new white Jewish lawyer in the Louima case, Sanford Rubenstein. And Sharpton said to him, 'Do you mean *Brother* Rubenstein?'"

I was pleasantly surprised. His comments made me feel a whole lot better about the problems I'd been anticipating as the result of my encounters with Thomas and Figueroux.

We had planned a prayer vigil at Kennedy airport the night before the march, when Louima's nine-year-old daughter was due to fly in from Haiti—Congressman Towns having finally secured the needed approval from the U.S. government for her immigration to America. The press had gathered to witness her arrival, but the family decided this wasn't a good time for her to talk to reporters, exhausted as she was from the long plane ride. As fate would have it, that very same day Abner had developed an adhesion in his intestines, and was curled up in a fetal position in his hospital bed in excruciating pain. Emergency surgery was scheduled for that night.

At the vigil, I was approached by an AP reporter who startled me by demanding, "How do we know the daughter really came in? And how do we know it's true that Abner Louima is having emergency surgery? The hospital hasn't said anything about it.... Isn't this all just a ploy to build up the march?" Of course, it was all true—but her words reminded me of just how skeptical some journalists can be.

The next day, Samantha Louima finally did meet with the press. She stood on a chair and addressed the assembled reporters in French, showing amazing poise and grace for a nine-year-old. Clearly, she was her father's daughter.

On the day of the rally, I rode to Brooklyn's Prospect Park dressed in a suit and tie with a pair of sneakers on my feet. The last protest march I'd participated in had been the march for democracy in Haiti, and I wanted to be sure I was wearing something comfortable to walk in. When I got there, it was immediately clear that the rally was going to be very substantial. By my estimate, there were tens of thousands of people massed at the rally's starting point in front of the Prospect Park Civil War memorial— many of them carrying posters or waving toilet plungers to symbolize the stick used to attack Louima in the station house bathroom. Looking at the memorial, with its two columns topped by bronze eagles with wings aloft, I reflected on the irony: We were gathered at this monument honoring the defenders of the Union—the men who had finally defeated slavery in America—and yet, almost 140 years later, here we were, still fighting for the full protection and safety of our nation's African-American citizens.

As I got out of my car, I spotted Reverend Al Sharpton standing near one of the police barricades. I walked up to him, stuck out my hand, and said, "Reverend Sharpton, I'd like to introduce myself—*I'm Brother Rubenstein!*"

At that moment, the crowd began to stir and move down Flatbush Avenue toward Manhattan. I don't remember if I linked arms with Sharpton or vice versa, but there we suddenly were, arm in arm, leading the march, with Abner Louima's brother and cousins alongside us. We marched together like that for the next several hours, down Flatbush Avenue, over the Brooklyn Bridge, and into Manhattan. As we walked, Sharpton gave me a one-to-one seminar on the issue of police brutality. He also explained to me the nature of broad-based social movements. "A movement often looks chaotic, but it isn't," he said. Gesturing at the spirited crowd spread out behind us, he added, "Movements run on passion. What else would make so many of these people take the day off from work to show up here and make their voices heard?"

It was a defining moment for me, personally and professionally. Not only did I discover that Sharpton was far from the anti-Semitic pariah that the press had portrayed him to be, but I also got to see his leadership skills in action: The marching route turned sharply at the entrance onto the Brooklyn Bridge, and in making the turn the crowd somehow split into two columns. Our side of the leading group fell behind the other half, and we needed to skirt around the side of the march—crossing some police barricades in the process—in order to get back to the front of the line. But when we attempted to do this, we were suddenly charged by a squad of helmeted police in full riot gear. As the police rushed forward some of the marchers, frightened and angry, began hurling insults at them.

Sharpton immediately moved to get the situation under control. "Hold it!" he shouted to the crowd. The marchers, responding to his exhortations, quickly calmed down. He then proceeded to explain to the commanding officer that we were simply trying to get to the front of the march. The police relented, and let us get where we needed to go. Sharpton, I realized, had deftly defused a potentially explosive situation—to the benefit of everyone involved.

The march proceeded peacefully from there. When we arrived at City Hall, where the speaker's platform had been set up, the assembled crowd stretched down Broadway as far as the eye could see. The day before, I'd asked Abner Louima what I should say to the marchers. He replied, "Tell them, 'Kimbala.'" It was a Creole word, he explained, that meant, "Stay strong."

I could hardly believe it: Here Abner was, lying in a hospital bed about to face emergency surgery, with so many people praying for his recovery—yet he was the one telling *them* to stay strong. It was a true measure of the man.

Now, I stood before the thousands of protestors and

announced, "Abner Louima says to you: *Kimbala!*" A giant roar erupted from the crowd.

The march was a huge success. For many people, the mass protest against what had happened to Abner crystallized their fears about being victimized by police brutality. I'll never forget a conversation I had at the first annual dinner of Sharpton's National Action Network, which took place a few months after the Louima rally. During the cocktail hour, an important black media mogul took me aside and told me, "I'm a very successful multimillionaire, and the police know who I am. But to them, my teenage son is just another black youth. When he walks out the door, I'm more afraid of him getting hurt at the hands of the police than at the hands of a common criminal."

In serving as Louima's lawyer, I was learning something that, as a white, middle-class American, I'd been unaware of: There exists a very real fear among members of America's black community that their children may suffer violence from the police—a fear that was epitomized by the horrific experience that Louima had endured, simply because he was in the wrong place at the wrong time.

In New York City, these fears had intensified in the 1990s, during Rudy Giuliani's time as mayor. There was a general feeling that Giuliani had created an atmosphere in which the police felt they could get away with anything. This sense was palpable at the Louima rally, where many of the posters featured anti-Giuliani rhetoric.

Giuliani, who was in the midst of a reelection campaign, was well aware of this sentiment. In fact, it was reported at the time that his advisers had been worrying about just this kind of incident—a high-profile case of police brutality that would give ammunition to the mayor's critics. Faced with these political pressures, along with the fact that what had happened to Louima was such a blatant act of gratuitous cruelty, Giuliani abandoned what many believed to be his usual practice of giving the benefit of the doubt to any police officer accused of wrongdoing. When reports of Louima's torture first surfaced in the press, the mayor immediately made a statement calling the charges "shocking to any decent human being," adding that, if proven to be true, they "should result in the severest penalties, including substantial terms of imprisonment and dismissal from the force." That same day, Giuliani, along with police commissioner Howard Safir, visited Louima in the hospital, then met with leaders of New York's Haitian community to assure them that if any police officers turned out to have been involved, they would be quickly arrested.

Giulani was as good as his word: Following news that an unnamed police officer had come forward with information about which officers had taken part in the assault, Justin Volpe, a 25-year-old patrolman, was arrested and charged with aggravated sexual abuse and first-degree assault. The NYPD also announced that Officer Thomas Bruder—Volpe's partner on that fateful night—had been transferred to desk duty.

The next day, Comissioner Safir cleaned house at the headquarters of the 70th precinct, announcing that the top two supervisors were being reassigned to different precincts. Safir also suspended the desk sergeant who had been on duty the night of the assault, and placed ten other police officers on desk duty until further notice.

Volpe was quickly indicted by a Brooklyn grand jury for aggravated sexual abuse and first-degree assault. The grand jury also indicted another officer, 32-year-old Charles Schwarz, on the same charges, for allegedly holding Louima down while Volpe sodomized him with the stick.

Three days later, two other police officers, Bruder and Thomas Wiese, were formally charged with the crime of beating Louima in their patrol car on the way to the precinct house. While several other officers would also eventually be charged in the course of the investigation, these four would remain the central figures in the Louima case over the next five years, as it made its complicated way through the criminal justice system.

The Arrival of the Dream Team

On October 10, 1997—almost exactly two months after he was attacked in the 70th Precinct house bathroom—Abner Louima was finally released from Brooklyn Hospital. Several weeks later, it was announced that super-lawyer Johnnie Cochran and his two New York-based partners, Barry Scheck and Peter Neufeld, were joining Louima's legal team. Suddenly Louima was being represented by The Dream Team, and the press had a field day with the news. The *New York Times* reported that "a relatively obscure squad of Brooklyn lawyers...now...find themselves sharing the case with three big-name colleagues, including perhaps the most famous lawyer in America today, Johnnie L. Cochran Jr."

While I'd never thought of myself as "obscure," I was more than happy to join forces with three such experienced attorneys, including the legendary Cochran. His untimely death in March of 2005 was a huge loss to the legal community and to the world. His reputation as one of the nation's top lawyers was richly deserved: Not only was Cochran brilliant on his feet in the courtroom, but he was also a genius at coming up with a creative and effective strategy when confronted with a difficult situation.

Over the years, I was privileged to work with Johnnie on a number of cases in different parts of the country, and had a chance to see his courtroom brilliance firsthand. A perfect example of this was a case in which Johnnie and I were jointly representing the four middle-aged children of an elderly Caribbean woman who had died in an automobile accident. For some reason, the driver of the other car lost control of her car and veered onto the wrong side of the road, smashing into the elderly woman's car and killing her.

The case, in which we were seeking damages for wrongful death from the insurance company of the young woman who had caused the accident, was being tried before an arbitrator. The driver of the car at fault, a young, very pretty white college student, was sobbing on her mother's shoulder as she related what had happened. She clearly felt terrible about having caused the death of this woman. While her remorse spoke well for her sense of humanity, I was concerned that the sympathies of the arbitrator would now begin to shift over from my four middle-aged clients to the young lady who'd caused their mother's death.

Concerned, I looked over at Johnnie. Sensing my thoughts, he nodded at me—a nod that said: "Don't worry, I'll take care of things when we get our chance during summation." When our turn came to sum up our case before the judge, Cochran glanced at the woman and her mother, and then said slowly, "In times of emotional distress, this young girl still has her mother to turn to." Then he pointed to the four adult children of the dead woman. *"They no longer have their mother."* In two sentences, he had completely taken the steam out of any sympathy that may have been building for the young driver and put the focus of the case back where it belonged: on the damages that these grown children were entitled to. That same day, the case was settled for a substantial and appropriate sum of money.

Another case in which Johnnie and I were involved, Johnnie on the legal side, and me on the movement side working with Reverend Sharpton, involved an incident that took place on the New Jersey Turnpike on April 23, 1998. Four young men—three African-Americans and one Hispanic-American—had been driving down the Turnpike, headed from New York City to a basketball clinic in North Carolina, when their van was pulled over by New Jersey state troopers. According to press reports, the New Jersey state police already had a notorious reputation at that time for disproportionately targeting drivers of color and pulling them over. In this case, however, as further reported in the press, when the driver of the van accidentally put the gearshift into reverse and the van started rolling backward, the troopers lost all control and began firing their guns blindly into the vehicle. They ended up shooting a total of 11 rounds, hitting and seriously injuring three of the four passengers.

The case of the New Jersey Four marked the first time that the term "racial profiling" was used in the public arena. Reverend Al Sharpton was involved in the case from the very beginning. Several days after the shooting, he held a press conference asking then-New Jersey Governor Christie Whitman for an apology and a plan to end racial profiling, and threatening civil disobedience if both weren't forthcoming. In late May, true to his words, Reverend Sharpton led a sit-in by several hundred people at the site of the shooting. The demonstration shut down traffic on the Turnpike. "Until then, the only other time the Turnpike had ever been shut down was for a hurricane," Rev told me later. "This was another kind of hurricane."

Reverend Sharpton was arrested as a result of the sit-in. Meanwhile, as reported in the media, the state authorities tried to stonewall charges of profiling at first, claiming that the troopers' radar had caught the van speeding, and that New Jersey state police never engaged in racial profiling. But the shooting, which occurred not long after the police killing of Amadou Diallo in New York City, sparked such an unprecedented outpouring of public anger that Governor Whitman's administration was soon forced to address the situation. First, the state admitted that the troopers didn't even have a radar gun in their car. They then announced there would be an official investigation into the actions of the troopers. In June, two months after the shooting, Whitman went further, decreeing that from that point onward all state police cruisers would be equipped with video cameras. "Clearly with the most recent incident…it was something we should move forward with," she told the press at the time the new policy was unveiled.

The following spring, almost a year to the day after the Turnpike shooting, Whitman announced that a new two-month survey had revealed that the New Jersey state police were indeed engaging in racial profiling. The survey confirmed the findings of a New Jersey Superior Court judge's findings in a 1996 case, in which the judge threw out criminal charges against 17 black motorists after hearing six months of evidence, including a 40-month survey showing that African-Americans made up 46 percent of all traffic stops on a 26-mile stretch of Turnpike, despite the fact that they comprised only 13 percent of the drivers.

In December of 1999, the state of New Jersey reached a consent decree with the U.S. Department of Justice in which it officially agreed to ban racial profiling and to make significant changes in how the state police were trained and supervised. It was a victory for civil rights and equal justice under the law—a victory that was facilitated by the activism of Reverend Sharpton.

It took several more years to wrap up all the legal proceedings around the case. Two state troopers who were originally charged with aggravated assault and, in one officer's case, attempted murder, ended up losing their jobs but serving no jail time after being allowed to plead guilty to lesser charges. Meanwhile, the state of New Jersey settled the lawsuit brought on behalf of the four young men for $12.9 million dollars.

Most important, though, was the fact that the battle against racial profiling had been joined once and for all. "Just as segregation was the civil rights battle of the nineteen-fifties, and voting rights and equal opportunity were the civil rights issues of the nineteen-sixties, the civil rights fight in the first part of the 21st century is going to be over racial profiling," Reverend Sharpton told me recently. "It's happening to people of color everywhere—on the highway, at the mall, even on the job. The movement against racial profiling really began with the New Jersey Turnpike shooting—which was the first incident that actually coined the term. Eventually racial profiling turned into a national issue, but it all started when we sat down in the middle of the New Jersey Turnpike."

In the years since that case, the efforts to spotlight the problem of racial profiling in New Jersey have produced changes that reverberated throughout the United States, as people across the nation began to realize just how pervasive the practice was. In 2000, a huge march, led by Reverend Sharpton—which I participated in—was held in Washington D.C. against racial profiling. In addition, then-president Bill Clinton hosted a White House conference focusing on the issue. State legislatures around the country also began to take up the cause against racial profiling—including the state of Illinois, where an anti-profiling bill was sponsored by an Illinois state legislator, relatively unknown at the time, named Barack Obama.

A few weeks after Cochran and his colleagues joined Louima's legal team, a long article about the case, written by Marie Brenner, appeared in *Vanity Fair* magazine. Brenner's piece was, in my opinion, relatively sympathetic to the accused officers—a couple of who appeared to have spoken to her at length (or had their lawyers speak for them). I couldn't say the same about her treatment of me, however. My guess is that Brenner was angry because I hadn't allowed Abner to be interviewed by her. It's always been my view that the client comes first, and I knew that Abner was going to be a crucial witness in the upcoming criminal trial and possibly a subsequent civil trial as well. I also knew that anything he said in an interview could later be used in court by the defense counsel during cross-examination to attack him. So I blocked the interview. Brenner responded by describing me in print as being "diminutive," and having "the personal style of a hammer." I accepted the insults, knowing that I'd done right by my client. Given the way she'd attacked me in print, who knows what Brenner would have written about Louima if he'd spoken to her?

In yet another outgrowth of the case, a public hearing on police violence was held on November 18, 1997 at Medgar Evers College in Crown Heights, Brooklyn. The hearing had been convened by Congressman John Conyers of Michigan, the senior Democrat on the House Judiciary Committee, together with the Center for Constitutional Rights, a non-profit group based in Manhattan. For several hours, a stream of ordinary people walked up to the microphone to relate how one of their loved ones had been victimized by police violence. It was an incredibly moving event. Zachary Carter, the U.S. Attorney for the Federal district that included Brooklyn, spoke eloquently about how difficult it was to prosecute police officers who perpetrated violence on innocent people. Eight Congressmen, including Conyers, were also in attendance. One person who was noticeably absent was Mayor Rudolph Giuliani, who earlier that day had called the hearing "a political rally."

With all of these events swirling around the case, my primary job was still to look out for the interests of my client. This involved staying in constant touch with Abner and serving as an ongoing source of support and advice as he prepared for the day when he would have to testify in court against his attackers. In the meantime, I was also kept busy deflecting the importunings of reporters like Marie Brenner, many of who were dying for a chance to interview my client.

Early on in the Louima case, I was eating dinner at a fashionable New York City restaurant when I ran into Judge Milton Mollen, a former chief judge of one of New York's appellate divisions—a very important appeals court—who was dining with Barbara Walters. They invited me over to their table for a drink. I explained to Walters that I was involved in the most high-profile case of my career, and asked her if she had any tips on handling the press. She gave me three simple rules to follow:

1. Always return reporters' phone calls.
2. Be honest with the press. If you can't talk about something, simply say, "I'm sorry, but I can't talk about that." (This, she explained, is basically a better version of "No comment.")
3. Don't let them bully you.

I was struck by how generous she was with her time and advice. Some time later, Barbara asked me if she could interview Abner for the first episode of her new television show, *The View*. After her kind advice, I was disappointed that I couldn't reciprocate—but I had to say no. As a witness in a major police brutality case, it simply wasn't in Abner's best interest to appear on national TV at that point. In general, there are both advantages and disadvantages to having your client speak out on television during a high profile case, and as a lawyer you need to balance them against each other. One advantage is that it provides a chance to get your client out in the public eye and to portray him in a positive light—so long as he doesn't discuss any details of the case. The major disadvantage, as mentioned earlier, is that if your client does slip up and say something specific about the case, it can be used against him later in court, particularly on cross-examination.

The most important rule in weighing the value of media appearances is this: *always do what's in your client's best interest*. For a lawyer, the corollary to this is: *don't be star-struck by the opportunity to appear in the national spotlight*. Otherwise, you run the risk of overdoing the publicity and not only hurting your client but also becoming the object of media criticism yourself. A perfect example of this is William Ginsburg, the lawyer who initially represented Monica Lewinsky, who was severely criticized by the media for his overexposure on national television as he raced from show to show in the days after news of the scandal first broke.

Occasionally, you inherit a situation that you have no control over. Prior to my involvement in the Louima case, a commitment had been made for Abner's wife and cousin to appear on *Nightline* with Ted Koppel. I did the best I could in the situation, negotiating an agreement stipulating that Koppel would only ask yes-no questions with regard to any specifics as to what was witnessed that night. Once the camera started rolling, however, the first thing out of Koppel's mouth was a narrative question to the cousin: "Could you tell me in your own words what happened?"

I had to stop the interview on the spot. Fortunately, it was being taped; we'll never know what would have happened if it was being shot live. I explained to Koppel and his producer that I was just doing my job, representing my client. Koppel was gracious—as he explained to me, he was just doing *his* job. Still, he didn't keep his word. From that day onward I never let another client of mine appear on his show, because I didn't trust him.

Meanwhile, the New York State court case went slowly forward. On November 20, an appeals court rejected a request by Justin Volpe's attorney, Marvyn Kornberg, that Volpe's trial be moved out of the New York region. Then, on December 15, Kornberg asked that Volpe be tried separately from the other three officers. The attorney for Charles Schwarz had already made a similar request, which had been turned down. Clearly, there was some bad blood between the various defendants. That same day, the Brooklyn District Attorney's office turned over hundreds of pages of evidence to the defense lawyers. According to the *Times,* this evidence included "a police laboratory report saying that blood likely to have come from Mr. Louima was found on a glove that investigators say Officer Volpe borrowed shortly before torturing Mr. Louima in the station house bathroom."

Things were definitely not looking good for Volpe.

1997 turned into 1998. In mid-January, Louima caused a stir in the media when he voluntarily retracted his widely-reported assertion that, in the midst of the attack on him, one of the accused officers had shouted, "It's not Dinkins time—it's Giuliani time!" This was a critical moment, for it was the first time that Louima's credibility had been tarnished. As Louima explained it, he had gone along with the invented phrase on bad advice, to help insure that his plight drew the attention of the media. Now he wanted to set the record straight. By doing so, however, he risked having the tide of public opinion turn against him. Even more important, his misstatement would provide an opening in court to attack his credibility regarding his account of what was done to him, when and if he appeared on the witness stand to testify against the officers who had attacked him.

Naturally, I was besieged by reporters wanting to know what this turn of events meant as far as the case against Louima's attackers was concerned. At this crucial moment, Johnnie Cochran once again showed why he was such a superb advocate and brilliant strategist. I quickly huddled with Johnnie to find out how he thought we should deal with the situation. "Abner is still the victim," he said simply. "Whether the comment was or wasn't made by the police officer isn't important. What's important is that the public shouldn't lose sight of the fact that Abner was the *victim* of this torture."

I followed Johnnie's advice to the letter, and the storm of controversy surrounding Louima's retraction eventually blew over. Even though I was the one who ended up being quoted in most of the daily tabloids, it was Cochran's quick thinking that provided me with the appropriate comments to make under the circumstances—and it's Johnnie who deserves the credit for handling the crisis.

While the state prosecution inched forward, a Federal investigation was also continuing, pursuant to the possibility that Zachary Carter's U.S. Attorney office might take over the case from Brooklyn District Attorney Charles Hynes. There was a widespread feeling that this was almost certainly going to happen—in fact, people had been expecting the Feds to announce they were taking over the case for the past six months. Since it hadn't happened yet, many folks were starting to ask why the Federal investigation was taking so long.

In late February, the *New York Times* ran a piece about the delay. "Federal investigators and other state investigators say that the Federal inquiry has taken so long for several reasons," the paper reported. "One is that the Federal investigation has been wider in scope than the state effort, since Federal prosecutors have been trying to determine whether others should be charged with crimes besides the four officers who have been indicted in the state case.... Federal prosecutors have been trying to determine whether other officers should also be charged with crimes like failing to halt the alleged assault or trying to cover it up."

The *Times* added, "Another explanation for the time expended during the Federal effort, according to Federal investigators themselves, is that they are determined to be thorough in their inquiry to produce 'the highest degree of confidence that there is a case that will produce a conviction,' as one Federal investigator put it... For that reason, the prosecutors in the United States Attorney's office in Brooklyn who are conducting the Federal inquiry are said to have started from scratch, reportedly having their investigators re-interview all the witnesses who had been interviewed for the state inquiry."

The reason the Feds were being so careful was simple: If the accused parties were acquitted in a state trial, they could be tried again in Federal court for criminal civil rights violations. This has happened in a number of instances, including one very high-profile case in New York City involving police officer Francis Livotti, who killed a civilian named Anthony Baez with an illegal chokehold.

The reverse, however, is not true: If Federal prosecutors fail to get a conviction, the accused can't be retried in state court. That meant that a Federal trial would be the only opportunity any court would have of trying Volpe and the others for the assault on Louima—and the U.S. Attorney's office, led by Zachary Carter, was determined to get it right.

Three days later, on Feb. 26, 1998, the other shoe finally dropped: Carter and Hynes called a joint news conference to announce that the U.S. government was taking over the Louima case, and that Carter's office would be prosecuting the accused officers on Federal charges of violating Abner Louima's civil rights.

This was undoubtedly the single most important moment in the entire case. The decision had a number of very significant implications. For one thing, the Feds, in my opinion, have much better success than state prosecutors when it comes to cases of police misconduct. This is due in part to the fact that Federal prosecutors have unlimited resources, including use of the FBI. They also have more experienced career trial lawyers. Plus, a Federal case brings a guarantee of a jury trial, if the prosecutor wants one. In Federal court, the prosecutor and the defense both have to agree to waive a jury trial—as opposed to New York State law, where the defense lawyer can unilaterally opt to waive the right to a trial by jury. This meant that if the defendants in the Louima case had been tried in state court they could have opted for a judge-only trial, which might have given them a better shot at acquittal.

In addition, the Federal charges of violating Louima's civil rights carried much tougher maximum sentences than the state charges did. The Federal takeover also meant that the jury would be hearing the results of interviews by FBI agents—which, since lying to an FBI agent is a Federal crime itself, made it much more likely that the accused officers' colleagues on the force would break the "blue wall of silence" and be forthcoming about what they might have seen or heard that August night.

It was ironic that I found myself pleased when Charles "Joe" Hynes, District Attorney for King's County (the official name for the borough of Brooklyn) decided to give up the case, because he's a man I greatly admire, and who I believe the people of Brooklyn are fortunate to have as a prosecutor. I'm sure he would have done his best to convict those responsible for Louima's attack. Still, it was the right decision. Besides the four officers who had already been charged in state court, the Federal indictment named a fifth defendant in the case, Sergeant Michael Bellomo, who stood accused of helping to cover up the fact that Volpe had attacked and beaten another Brooklyn resident, Patrick Antoine, on the street shortly before returning to the precinct house where Louima was assaulted. Word was that Carter's office was looking at additional indictments, as well. Clearly, the Feds were intent on prosecuting not just the alleged attackers themselves, but any other police officers who conspired to help them hide what they'd done.

All five of the accused police officers pleaded not guilty; they were released on $100,000 bail apiece.

The Federal investigation continued on through the spring, summer and early fall. Finally, in September of 1998, the Federal judge assigned to the case, 80-year-old Eugene Nickerson, named a tentative start date for the trial of March 22, 1999.

A number of pretrial documents were unsealed in November, giving some hints of how the trial was likely to unfold. According to the *New York Times,* two of the documents contained statements that appeared to incriminate Volpe in the attack. One was a memo written by my colleagues, Johnnie Cochran and Peter Neufeld, detailing a statement made to them a year earlier by Officer Wiese, in which he told them that he had walked into the precinct house bathroom shortly after the attack and seen Abner Louima lying on the floor, his pants and underwear down around his ankles, with Volpe standing over him holding a stick covered with feces. According to the memo, Wiese also claimed Volpe told him later that night that Louima had defecated on himself.

It was unclear how much weight Wiese's statement would carry in a trial, since (as Volpe's defense lawyer Marvyn Kornberg immediately pointed out to the press) he had made a similar claim to police interviewers shortly after the attack, only to have it discounted after he failed a lie detector test. As to *why* Wiese had been talking to Cochran and Neufield, another newly unsealed document—a court filing by Wiese's lawyers—indicated that he had met with them in an attempt to persuade them to treat him as a witness rather than as a defendant in the civil case we had filed against the four officers.

The second document contained notes from an FBI interview with Officer Bruder, in which Bruder reportedly told agents that he had seen Volpe taking Louima into the bathroom shortly before the attack occurred, and that Volpe had later admitted striking Louima with a mop handle.

Three days after the release of the unsealed documents, there was another bombshell: The grand jury announced that they were expanding their indictment of Schwarz, Wiese and Bruder to include the charge of conspiracy—alleging that the three officers, along with unnamed others, had lied about certain events on the evening that Louima was attacked, in order to protect Schwarz from being implicated in the assault in the bathroom.

Naturally, the three men's defense lawyers denounced the new charge in the press. One called it "an attempt to pile up more dirt on the defendants," while another called it a "rather obvious attempt" by Federal prosecutors to prevent Wiese and Bruder from appearing as defense witnesses for Schwarz in the upcoming trial.

In yet another twist to the case, a month later, in mid-December, two additional police officers, Rolando Aleman and Franciso Rosario, were charged with lying to Federal investigators about having seen someone other than Volpe escorting Louima from the bathroom to the holding cell that August night. According to this new indictment, the two officers' motivation wasn't to protect Volpe specifically, but rather to avoid having to testify against Volpe in court and be labeled "rats" as a result. Once again, Kornberg, along with the lawyers representing the two officers, quickly complained to the press that the charges were intended to prevent the officers from testifying for the defense.

Clearly, the "blue wall of silence" was alive and well. Meanwhile, it was beginning to look like everyone was going to need scorecards to keep track of the legal proceedings in this increasingly complex case!

The "Blue Wall" Crumbles

On March 29, 1999, a year and a half after the attack on Louima, the jury selection for the Federal trial of Volpe, Schwarz, Wiese,

Bruder and Bellomo finally got underway. The previous month, Judge Nickerson had denied a request by the defense lawyers to move the trial out of New York City, and had also agreed to a request by prosecutors to allow the jurors in the case to remain anonymous—an approach that is sometimes used in especially controversial cases, to protect the jurors from any outside pressures that might affect their ability to weigh the testimony impartially. Nickerson had also rejected a number of requests by the various defense lawyers to have the five police officers tried separately, ruling that "Persons indicted together for crimes arising out of a similar series of acts or involving substantially the same evidence should generally be tried together."

On the morning of the 29th, more than 700 prospective jurors showed up at the Federal District Courthouse in Brooklyn, drawn not only from that borough but also from Queens, Staten Island and Long Island. The sidewalk outside was crawling with television crews and reporters. Most of the prospective jurors waved them away but a few stopped to give interviews, in direct violation of the instructions they'd received not to discuss the case with anybody. The defense lawyers got wind of this and filed a motion to dismiss the entire juror pool—a motion that Nickerson rejected a few days later, although he did slap a restraining order on the journalists covering the case, forbidding them from interviewing, photographing or sketching any potential jurors. At the same time, he turned down another request by the officers' defense lawyers to postpone the trial for at least four months on the grounds that media coverage had made it impossible for their clients to get a fair trial. "There must be 18 people among 785 who will be fair and impartial," said the judge—to which Volpe's defense lawyer quipped, "Hope springs eternal, Judge."

The jury selection was expected to take a month or more. In addition to answering oral questions put to them by the various lawyers in the case, the potential jurors also had to fill out a 40-page questionnaire containing 128 questions. This highly unusual step was a reflection of the huge notoriety surrounding the case. Among other things, the judge and the participating attorneys wanted to know exactly what each potential juror had gleaned from the media about the case, and what their views were regarding the way minorities were treated by the NYPD—an issue that had gained new prominence with the killing just a month earlier of Amadou Diallo, shot 19 times by police as he stood in the darkened entrance of his Brooklyn apartment building.

It took both teams of lawyers two weeks to wade through the 30,000 pages of questionnaire responses and compile lists of the candidates they wanted to have dismissed from the jury pool on the basis of their answers. After reviewing these lists and also taking into account his own evaluation of the responses, Judge Nickerson's next step would be to approve a preliminary panel of between 80 and 100 candidates, from which the final jury would hopefully be drawn.

After six days, Nickerson was more than halfway through this process, having approved 52 panel members, when Justin Volpe's father blew a gasket. Robert Volpe was a retired police detective who had become quite well known as the department's leading expert on art theft and forgeries. Obviously, the past year and half had been very tough on him. After Nickerson approved a 62-year-old man who had claimed during his courtroom interview to have serious memory problems, it proved too much for the senior Volpe. According to media reports, when reporters approached him outside the courthouse he exploded in rage, saying that the judge was "stacking the jury" and that his son was the victim of a "modern-day lynching." He also raised the issue of the arrests of officers Aleman and Rosario the previous December, asserting that "there's no difference between assassinating a witness…and falsely arresting someone to prevent him from telling the truth."

The truth was, the case against his son kept looking stronger and stronger as additional court filings were released to the public in the weeks leading up to the trial. Prosecutors had already indicated that they would be putting another police officer, Eric Turetzky, on the stand to testify against Volpe. Reportedly, Turetzky told investigators that he'd seen Volpe leading Louima away from the bathroom area with his pants down around his ankles.

Pretrial documents also hinted at the fact that defense lawyers would be introducing medical evidence to suggest that Louima's injuries had occurred as the result of anal intercourse before his arrest, rather than an assault with a stick. If so, it would be an incredibly cynical move—although it was one that I'd been anticipating for many months. From the very start of Louima's ordeal, when, according to news reports, the officers who escorted his ambulance to the hospital told the medical staff there that he'd been injured in a homosexual encounter, there had been hints that this argument might be floated in an attempt to explain away the injuries that Volpe had inflicted. Indeed, this was one of my concerns in arranging the press coverage of Abner's daughter as she was being admitted into the U.S.—to show to the world that this was a married man with young children, and hardly the type of person to engage in homosexual activity in a nightclub.

The exhaustive process continued to inch forward for several more weeks. A panel of 85 candidates was chosen, and a second round of interviews then commenced to select actual jurors from this group. Finally, in early May, the last juror was seated. The jury that would try the five police officers was made up of eight whites, one black, and three self-identified Hispanics—seven males and five females—plus six alternates. Pursuant to Judge Nickerson's earlier ruling, all eighteen would remain strictly anonymous throughout the course of the trial.

On May 4, the trial got underway. As Louima's personal lawyer, I had been asked by the prosecutors not to attend the proceedings. They didn't want to give the lawyers for the accused officers a chance to point at me in the courtroom during their opening statement and say, "This case is all about the money—the lawyer who is suing the city for millions of dollars on Louima's behalf is sitting right there."

As it was, Volpe's lead lawyer, Marvyn Kornberg, made that argument anyway without me being present, stating in his opening remarks that since Louima had filed a lawsuit for some $150 million dollars he had "150 million reasons to curb the truth." As expected, Kornberg also brought up the theory that Louima had somehow gotten his injuries from consensual sex with a man—telling the jury that he would be introducing medical evidence that Abner's internal injuries "were not consistent with the nonconsensual insertion of an object," and that he also had evidence that Louima's feces was found to contain the DNA of another man on the night in question.

The fact that these charges were preposterous on their face, and that the prosecutors had already indicated they had a medical expert who would testify that Louima's severe injuries could *only* have been caused by a blunt object inserted into his rectum, didn't seem to deter Kornberg. Seeking to undermine Louima's credibility, the defense lawyers also used their opening statements to hammer home the fact that Louima had lied when he made his famous claim that one of the officers had shouted "It's Giuliani time."

Kenneth Thompson, a member of the prosecution team who made the government's opening statement, also addressed this point in an attempt to defuse it, admitting that Louima's false claim had been a "foolish lie," told by Abner "because he thought it would bring attention to what was done to him." Thompson also detailed what Louima had been through that night in August 1997—how he had been beaten twice on the way to the police station where he was then beaten a third time. "That third beating was far more vicious than the first two beatings," Thompson went on. "And that's because inside that bathroom, Abner Louima suffered more than just a beating. Ladies and gentlemen, Abner Louima was tortured in that bathroom, and his torture was cruel and it was simply inhumane."

Thompson also revealed for the first time that the person who had punched Volpe in front of the Club Rendez-Vous—sparking Volpe's violent rampage—was Abner Louima's cousin, Jay Nicholas, who Volpe apparently mistook to be Louima.

Louima took the witness stand on day three of the trial. For over three hours, at the prodding of prosecutors, he recounted what had happened to him that night, explaining how, after he was already crying from a kick in the groin, one of the officers in the precinct house bathroom had held him down while another thrust an object first into his rectum and then into his mouth, telling him that it was his own feces he was tasting. One of the prosecutors then asked if the man who attacked him was present in the courtroom. "He's right there," Louima said, and he pointed a shaking finger directly at Justin Volpe.

Next came the defense attorneys' cross-examination of Louima, which lasted for the better part of two days. It was every bit as tough as we had expected, but Louima never wavered. As the lawyers pressed him to describe exactly where and when he'd been at each point of the evening, where he'd been punched, and exactly who said what to whom, he answered every question slowly and cautiously, sticking to the facts as he had already outlined them, and keeping his responses brief and to the point. Any time he was uncertain about a question he would request that the lawyers repeat it, to be sure he understood exactly what he was being asked. The defense was so frustrated by his performance that, at one point, they actually accused him of being coached by some unnamed person sitting in the courtroom!

There was one thing that the defense never brought up, however—and that was the suggestion, alluded to by Kornberg in his opening statement, that Louima's injuries might have been caused by consensual sex. They obviously decided to abandon this line of attack. It seemed to me to be a wise decision. Jurors are no fools: They know when a lawyer goes over the line in trying to discredit a witness, and they certainly take that back to the jury room while conducting their deliberations.

As for Justin Volpe's father, Robert, the retired art detective, he seemed to think this omission represented some sort of strategy by the defense. "It's not an oversight," he was quoted as telling reporters after Louima had finished for the day—adding, "You're at the beginning of the movie. Let the movie play."

A week into the trial, whatever hopes Volpe might have had of persuading the jury that he was being falsely accused began to

crumble. On May 12, Eric Turetzky (who had recently been pro-
moted to detective and transferred to the NYPD's Department of
Internal Affairs) took the stand and described how he had seen
Justin Volpe leading Abner Louima from the bathroom that night:
Louima with his pants down below his knees, and Volpe oddly
hunched over, his uniform in disarray, and—most damning of all—
holding a two-to-three-foot-long stick that appeared to be part of
a broken handle of a broom or mop. After depositing Louima in a
holding cell, said Turetzky, Volpe came back down the hall, "holding the stick and displaying it to us, waving it in the air and banging
it against the wall."

Turetzky's testimony against a fellow cop was a stunning
breach of the legendary "blue wall of silence." The defense team
went after him hard, trying to discredit his motivation for testifying as being pure self-interest and nothing more. The next witness
to take the stand, however, was Mark Schofield, another police officer who had been in the precinct house that night. Schofield testified that he had seen Volpe carrying a "stick-like object" toward the
bathroom shortly before the attack on Louima, and had then proceeded to lend Volpe a pair of leather gloves—and that when Volpe
returned the gloves a short time later, they were covered in fresh
blood. Again, Kornberg and the other defense lawyers went after
Schofield aggressively, getting him to admit, among other things,
that the object he'd seen Volpe carrying could well have been an
ordinary nightstick.

The final blow to Volpe's defense came two days later, when a
surprise witness took the stand. Sergeant Kenneth Warwick had
been on a list of witnesses scheduled to testify, but no one—including, apparently, Volpe's attorneys—knew that his testimony
was going to be so damaging to the defense. Warwick recounted

hearing Volpe boast, "I took a man down tonight," before going on to describe in detail about how he had taken a stick and "put it four or five inches" into Louima's rectum. According to Warwick, Volpe then took him into the bathroom to show him the stick Volpe had used in the attack, and later pointed the stick at Warwick and asked if he could see Louima's feces on it.

Kornberg's cross-examination of Warwick was slated to begin the following morning. To the astonishment of almost everyone, however, Kornberg announced that he had no questions for the sergeant. He may as well have stood up then and there and waved a white flag, for it was clear that Volpe's defense had been left in tatters and that his only hope at this point was to strike some kind of deal with the prosecution. Instead, yet another officer, Michael Schoer, took the stand and told a similar tale of how Justin Volpe had shown him a broken stick with a brown stain on it, which Volpe had explained was from human feces. Again, Kornberg had no questions for the witness.

The next day, the courthouse was buzzing with rumors that Kornberg had sought a plea deal for his client, in which Volpe would provide investigators with new information in exchange for leniency—and that the offer had been rejected by U.S. Attorney Zachary Carter's office.

The weekend came and went. Monday, May 24, was devoted to the testimony of the trauma surgeon who had operated on Louima, who explained how Abner's various injuries lined up perfectly, indicating that they were caused by the same blunt object, and of investigators who testified about finding bloodstains in the squad car where Louima had allegedly been beaten by police following his arrest. By 3:45, the defense had had enough. Kornberg asked for a private bench conference with Judge Nickerson, in which he informed the judge that Justin Volpe was prepared to plead guilty the following day to the charge of sexually assaulting Abner Louima with a broken broom handle.

According to news reports, Volpe, at his own request, spent his last night of freedom in Staten Island visiting with his parents and girlfriend. The next day, it seemed as if all of New York City had turned out to see him enter his guilty plea. The courtroom was packed to capacity.

As part of his agreement to plead guilty, Volpe was required to give a detailed account of his actions in the early morning hours of August 9, 1997. Now he stood before the court with a sheet of paper in his hand and began to read from it. First, he described how he'd been struck by someone who he mistakenly thought was Louima in front of the Club Rendez-Vous. The next time he saw Louima, he said, was in the patrol car that would take Abner back to the precinct house.

Then came the moment of truth. He testified, as reported in the New York press: "While in the bathroom at the precinct, in the presence of another officer, I sodomized..."—here he paused and took a breath before continuing—"...Mr. Louima by placing a stick in his rectum. I then threatened to kill him if he told anybody."

He went on to add an intriguing, if ambiguous, detail: "While I was in the bathroom," said Volpe, "there was another police officer in the bathroom with me. That police officer saw what was going on, did nothing to stop it. It was understood from the circumstances that that police officer would do nothing to stop me or report it to anyone."

He'd concluded his statement, but Judge Nickerson wanted to hear more: "When you put the stick up towards his face, having shoved it into his rectum, was [this] a part of your effort to humiliate him?" asked the judge.

"I was in shock at the time, Your Honor," Volpe replied. "...I couldn't believe what happened...I was mad."

"You intended to humiliate him?" repeated the judge.

"Yes," said the defendant.

The hearing lasted 45 minutes, after which Volpe was led out of the courtroom in custody. Abner Louima wasn't there to hear his attacker confess, but his cousin, Samuel Nicolas, was. Afterwards, Nicolas spoke to reporters outside the courthouse, telling them "We'd just like to thank God for keeping Abner alive." He added that he and the rest of Abner's family were looking forward "for the rest of justice to be done."

Volpe's sentencing was postponed until an unspecified later date. He still risked a maximum sentence of life imprisonment without parole; but by pleading guilty and taking responsibility for his crime, Volpe had opened the door for the judge to show some leniency. According to Federal sentencing guidelines his sentence could conceivably be reduced to 25 to 30 years—still a long time to be incarcerated, but a far sight better than a lifetime behind bars.

Besides Louima, some other people were also conspicuously absent from the courtroom that day: the members of the jury. Because the trial would continue for Volpe's four co-defendants, it was essential that the jurors' evaluation of their cases remained untainted by Volpe's guilty plea. Ordinarily in this type of situation, the jurors wouldn't even be told the defendant had pled guilty. Instead, they'd simply be informed that he or she would no longer be appearing in court, and told not to infer anything from this abrupt vanishing act.

As it turned out, the prosecution and all but one of the defense lawyers joined together in requesting that Judge Nickerson tell the jury about Volpe's plea, and the judge agreed. It was a wise decision, since otherwise speculation would have run wild inside the juror's box. Besides, the jurors—who weren't sequestered—would very likely have found out about the guilty plea anyway.

With Volpe gone, the rest of the trial sped by. Rather than take away the three chairs that Volpe and his two lawyers had occupied, the remaining defendants chose to let the chairs sit there empty. It was a way of distancing themselves from Volpe. Throughout the trial, according to press reports, his co-defendants had studiously avoided speaking to or even looking at Volpe, apparently for the same reason.

The prosecution took just two additional days to wrap up its case. Of the four remaining defendants, the one who had the most at stake was Schwarz, who was accused of restraining Louima while Volpe assaulted him in the restroom. Two of the police officers who testified had placed Schwarz walking Louima down the hall to the restroom, his pants around his ankles. This, together with Louima's testimony that the officer who had driven him to the precinct house that night (which police records showed had been Schwarz) was also the one who held him down in the restroom, added up to a serious case against Schwarz.

The case against Wiese and Bruder rested primarily on Abner's own testimony, along with the fact that Abner's blood had been found in the patrol car that brought him in; meanwhile, the evidence against Sergeant Bellomo was largely indirect. Apparently their defense lawyers felt they had all done they needed to do during their intensive cross-examinations of the prosecution witnesses: When it came time to present their cases, Bruder's lawyer passed completely, while the other lawyers called only a handful of character witnesses between them. None of the defendants chose to take the witness stand themselves.

Now it was up to the jury to decide the fate of the four accused officers. After 18 hours of deliberations spread over two days, the twelve jurors sent word that they'd reached a consensus on the various charges.

Up until then I'd stayed away from the trial at the request of the prosecutors. On the day the verdict was announced, however, I felt it was appropriate to end my state of invisibility and show up in the courtroom. Even though I wasn't one of the lawyers prosecuting the case, I felt the same nervous rush of adrenaline that I get when I'm waiting for a jury to deliver their verdict in a case that I've tried. The jurors filed into the courtroom, and the verdicts were announced: Charles Schwarz was found guilty on the count of violating Abner Louima's civil rights by assisting in Volpe's assault with the broom handle. The three other officers were acquitted of all charges.

Interestingly enough, however, this didn't end the courtroom ordeal for the acquitted Wiese and Bruder—or for Schwarz, for that matter. Because the judge had granted a severance for one of the counts of the indictment—the charge of conspiring to obstruct justice—the three officers would now have to stand trial again on this outstanding count. The Louima case was far from over.

Filled with mixed feelings, I left the Federal courthouse. As I walked along the sidewalk, a New York Police Department van sped past and someone inside thrust an arm out through the open window. From inside the van, almost like a football cheer, I heard the loud chant: *"N…Y…P…D!"*

Hearing what was clearly intended as a cheer of victory really shook me up. It was incredibly disheartening to me that, after all the time and effort that had gone into this trial, and despite the fact that two officers had been convicted of a horrendous crime, the underlying message—namely, that what had happened to Abner Louima was absolutely unacceptable—still didn't seem to have filtered down to the rank and file.

No Simple Endings

The unresolved legal aspects of the Louima case continued to wind through the Federal justice system. That summer, Charles Schwarz's lawyer moved to have Schwarz's conviction overturned, based on Volpe's claim that Wiese, not Schwarz, had been in the bathroom during the attack on Louima, but had merely watched the assault without participating (Wiese himself had maintained that he entered the bathroom only briefly, after the attack had already occurred, and saw Volpe alone with Louima). Judge Nickerson dismissed the motion, noting that the defense had known about this claim at the time of the trial, but had chosen not to call Volpe to the witness stand—understandably so, since Volpe's credibility was nil at that point.

In December of 1999, Volpe was sentenced by Nickerson to 30 years in jail. Two months later, on February 7, 2000, after a month-long jury-selection process, Schwarz, Wiese and Bruder went on trial for a second time, on the Federal charge of conspiring to obstruct justice. Once again, Judge Nickerson would be presiding. The actual trial lasted three weeks, with the main evidence consisting of some 60 phone calls made between the three defendants in the days following the attack on Louima. The prosecutors asserted that these phone calls were part of an effort to cover up Schwarz's role in holding down Louima while Volpe assaulted him. Volpe, Schwarz and Wiese all appeared as witnesses to testify that Schwarz had never been in the bathroom that night. (Schwarz himself claimed that at the time of the attack, he was checking his patrol car for possible contraband that Louima might have stashed there.)

The key moment in this second trial may have come at the very end, when Judge Nickerson gave his final instructions to the jurors before sending them off to deliberate. Among other things, he told them they could find the defendants guilty of conspiracy even if they weren't convinced that Schwarz had actually been in the bathroom. After deliberating over five days, the jury announced that they'd found all three officers guilty as charged—a verdict that carried a maximum prison sentence of five years.

In June of 2000, Nickerson sentenced Schwarz to a prison term of 15 years and eight months for his assault and conspiracy convictions, while Wiese and Bruder each got five-year sentences for conspiracy.°

That same month, in the third trial resulting from the Louima case, a Federal jury found Officer Franciso Rosario guilty of lying to Federal investigators when he claimed not to have been in the cell area of the 70th Precinct house following the attack on Louima. The previous April, Rosario's colleague, Officer Rolando Aleman, had pled guilty to a similar charge. Rosario and Aleman

---

° Two years later, an appeals court overturned Schwarz's assault conviction and called for a retrial, ruling that his lawyer, who also had a contract to represent the PBA, had been unable to represent Schwarz adequately due to this inherent conflict of interest. The same court threw out the conspiracy convictions of Schwarz, Wiese and Bruder on technical grounds. Schwarz then went on to stand trial a third time, this time on a charge of perjury for lying about his role in leading Louima to the bathroom, and was convicted. He eventually agreed to accept a five-year prison sentence for the perjury charge, and never went through a retrial on the charge of assisting in Volpe's assault on Louima.

would eventually be sentenced to three and two years' probation, respectively. At last, it appeared the book was closed on the criminal charges stemming from the Louima case.

Not long after the conclusion of the second criminal trial of Schwarz, Wiese and Bruder, I received an invitation to meet with the New York City Corporation Counsel in his office to discuss the civil suit Abner's legal team had filed on his behalf against the city and the Police Benevolent Association. The counsel, Michael Hess, was someone whose name I'd seen in print, but I'd never actually met him. In fact, I didn't even know what he looked like! When I got to his office, I explained to Hess that I'd been authorized by my colleagues, Cochran, Scheck and Neufeld, to negotiate on behalf of the legal team. In response, Hess told me that the city was serious about negotiating a settlement. We began to discuss numbers, but didn't make much progress.

After a second, similar meeting also failed to move the ball forward very far, our legal team made a collective decision that the best way to proceed was to get the courts involved. We contacted Sterling Johnson, the Federal district judge assigned to the case, and he in turn gave his magistrate judge, Cheryl Pollak, the task of engaging all the key parties in negotiations. Her involvement was crucial: up to that time we'd been negotiating only with the city, even though the PBA was also named as one of the defendants. Judge Pollak was able to bring them to the table as well.

The settlement talks went on over many weeks in the judge's chambers, sometimes lasting late into the night, in which case we'd occasionally have Chinese food delivered from a local restaurant (which the judge made sure everyone paid for out of their own pockets). The talks were broken into two phases: Our first negotiations were with a team of lawyers from the city. Eventually, the city agreed to settle the part of the lawsuit brought against them for $7.125 million dollars—which at the time was, as far as I know, the largest amount New York City had ever agreed to pay to settle a police brutality lawsuit.

In the next phase, we entered into negotiations with the attorney representing the Police Benevolent Association. After a good deal of back and forth, we reached agreement on a $1.625 million settlement. It was the first time in history that a police union had agreed to pay damages to a victim of police misconduct.

The cash settlements were put on the record under oath before the judge. But the whole deal still hinged on whether we could come to an agreement with the city and the PBA regarding equitable relief—a term that refers to non-monetary concessions. One of the conditions that Louima was insisting on was some sort of substantive change in the way policing is done in New York City. In his and my view, this case wasn't just about money—it was also about improving the system in a way that would help prevent others from suffering the way Abner had.

As the settlement talks stretched into 2001, the nature of this equitable relief proved to be a sticking point. The PBA was very reluctant to do anything that made it appear they were giving in to pressure, while Abner was very serious about his demand for change. This sort of situation required a creative solution. Sometimes, I've found, you have to think outside the box to fashion a settlement that manages to satisfy all the parties. In the Louima suit, the agreement we finally hammered out was this: The PBA would agree to hire an independent outside lawyer to advise police officers who are involved as witnesses in a situations involving police brutality, rather than force them to consult with the regular

PBA criminal lawyers. This would help remove a major obstacle for those who wanted to break the "blue wall of silence."

However—and here was the catch—this change in policy wouldn't be linked specifically to the Louima settlement. Instead, we agreed that the police union would state that this was a change they were planning on making anyway, since that was their position. Meanwhile, we would take the position that the policy shift had actually occurred as a result of the settlement process. Whoever ultimately got the credit didn't really matter: The important thing was that the change happened, and that my client got the equitable relief he was seeking.

This new policy continues to this day, as do other key policy changes that occurred in the aftermath of the Louima case—particularly the city's commitment to end its "48-hour rule," which prevents administrative investigators from questioning police officers involved in alleged misconduct until 48 hours after the incident occurred.

The deal having been struck, we went before the press and announced the terms of the agreement. Naturally, the media focused on the fact that it was New York City's largest payout ever for a police brutality case, as well as the first time that a police union had ever paid damages to a victim of police brutality.

A decade later, I continue to be close with Abner Louima. He now resides in Florida with his wife and three children, working in the field of real estate investment. My respect and admiration for Abner only increased when he came to New York in 2006 to participate in a protest march over the Sean Bell shooting, in which Bell was killed by police in a hail of 50 bullets on the morning of his wedding day, a trip that included a hospital bedside visit to Joseph

Guzman, who had been wounded in the same attack—which undoubtedly reminded Abner of his own ordeal.

Recently, on the tenth anniversary of his torture attack, Abner recalled how I had told him when we first met that I would stand with him every step of the way and that when it was all over, we would be friends. "You told me this," he said to me, "and, just as you said, we remain friends today."

Around this time, the *New York Daily News* asked Abner to write an op-ed piece reflecting on what had transpired in the ten years since his attack. In the piece, he wrote in part:

> ...I think you will understand when I say that I try never to go back and think about what happened to me that night. I prefer to look forward.... After what happened to me, I consider myself lucky to be alive. For this reason, I enjoy and hold precious every second of my life.
>
> I also remain very involved in the cause of trying to change our system, so that what happened to me will never happen to my son, to anyone else's son. In my own case, I felt partial justice was done. Two of my attackers were incarcerated; one went to jail for 30 years.
>
> But others went free.
>
> In much the same way, I feel we have made some progress in reducing police brutality over the past 10 years, but I also believe there is still a lot to be done....
>
> When I was attacked, I was afraid that no one would pay any attention to what the police had done to me. Today, thanks to increased public awareness, I hope that if the police attack and harm an innocent person, it will not be met with silence. Also, as a result of the media attention surrounding my case, I hope many police officers will now think twice before committing a violent

act. But, unfortunately, I know some members of the police force still don't get it.

The reason for this, I believe, has to do with the way our justice system is set up. As long as local district attorneys are responsible for prosecuting police who commit criminally violent acts, there is a flaw in our system. This is because the D.A.s, as well-intentioned as they may be, still depend on the police to make the cases they prosecute, and they run the risk of alienating police departments by aggressively pursuing cases of police brutality.

The only way the police will ever be held truly accountable for their actions is by changing the system. We need to pass new legislation in New York State and nationwide, requiring that all police brutality cases be referred to either an independent state prosecutor or a Federal prosecutor, instead of being handled by local district attorneys. Until this happens, we cannot expect any significant improvement, because there will always be police officers who believe they can get away with attacks like the one I suffered.

In the meantime, for as long as my voice is needed, I will continue to speak out on behalf of those who have lost their lives to police violence. It makes me sick to know that innocent people are still being hurt and killed by the police. It's time we all said, "Enough is enough."

CHAPTER FOUR

BOMBS OVER VIEQUES

Slavery in the Desert

THE STORY OF MY involvement with the issue of the Navy's ongoing bombardment of the Puerto Rican island of Vieques actually begins in the troubled African nation of Sudan. In April of 2001, I accompanied Reverend Al Sharpton there to witness first-hand the horror of the Sudanese slave trade. This modern-day slavery is a grim offshoot of the civil conflict that's been simmering in that country for decades between the Sudanese government, based in Sudan's Muslim-dominated northern region, and the Sudanese People's Liberation Army (SPLA), the collective name for the various rebel factions based in rural southern Sudan, where the people are mainly Christians and adherents of Africa's traditional animist religion.

While the current civil war dates back to 1983, the SPLA have been waging an on-again off-again war against the government for the past 50 years. As with so many conflicts around the world, the armed struggle in Sudan has a strong ethnic component: Sudan's north is largely Arab, while the south is made up of black Africans. Ever since the fighting flared up anew in the 1980s, militias from northern Sudan have been raiding villages in non-Muslim southern Sudan and abducting any women and children they can lay their hands on. These unfortunate victims are then hauled to the north and sold into slavery. Besides being held captive and forced to work for nothing, they are often subjected to physical and sexual violence by their captors.

It's hard to believe that something so evil is still going on in this day and age. Even more sickening is the fact that, like the *jinjaweed* who have been perpetrating genocidal violence against the people of Darfur, the Arabic militias involved in the abductions in southern Sudan have the tacit backing of the Sudanese government, who view the militias as proxy forces in their fight to contain the rebel movement.

Our trip had been set up in conjunction with a Swiss-based organization, Christian Solidarity International, that recovers people who have been sold into slavery by paying "raiders," who have stolen the slaves back from those who originally captured them. Our objective was not to endorse or criticize this practice but simply to fact-find, to see for ourselves what was going on. We flew to Switzerland and then from there to Nairobi, where we boarded a small plane for southern Sudan. We didn't have a permit from the Sudanese government to be in the country. Instead, we were there at the invitation of the rebels, who controlled large portions of southern Sudan. This meant that, from the perspective of the Sudanese government, we were consorting with the enemy.

We landed in Sudan and had barely stepped off the plane when there was a loud boom like a bomb going off. "We're under attack already!" I thought, and dove for the ground as fast as I could. It turned out to be a truck backfiring, but I still couldn't shake a feeling of nervousness.

That night we slept in tents pitched on the edge of a small Sudanese village, deep in the brush. The next morning, we took a pickup truck to the site where we'd been told the slaves were assembled. Halfway there, the truck broke down, and we ended up jogging and walking the last part of the way. As I trotted under the burning sun with the Rev beside me, I was reminded of how fast a runner he is—a fact that might surprise some people. Even though I'm a former marathon runner, Sharpton is significantly more fleet of foot than I am—something I'd learned several years before, when we were both running down the street after Patrick Dorismond's hearse after it got too far ahead of us in the march led by Reverend Sharpton from the funeral parlor, where Patrick's wake was held, to the church for Patrick's funeral.°

We arrived finally at a large clearing, where nearly a thousand slaves were gathered. They were all either women—many with babies in their arms—or young boys. The women were covered with visible scars from beatings they're received during their enslavement, and the infants they were carrying had all been born as a result of being raped by their captors. It was a barbaric sight. Even amid this human evidence of horrific cruelty, however, I was struck by a wonderful example of humanity: After these women were reunited with their husbands, I learned, the men would invariably raise these infants, born as the result of their wives' being raped, as their own.

As we stood there, we could see, before our eyes, money passing

---

° Patrick Dorismond was an innocent victim wrongly killed by police in New York City in 2000.

from the representatives of Christian Solidarity International to the raiders. It cost the group about thirty-five dollars to buy each person's freedom—less than you'd pay for dinner at a typical Manhattan restaurant.

After the payments had been made, I had an opportunity to address the now-former slaves. By coincidence, this particular day happened to fall in the middle of Passover, when the Jewish people commemorate how God freed them from their enslavement by the Egyptians. Picking up on this theme, I started to express my hope that someday the people of Sudan could also look back on slavery as a relic of the past.

As I was speaking, I felt someone poke me in the ribs. Without turning to see who it was, I motioned for the person to get away from me—how dare he interrupt me in mid-speech? Then I heard the voice of our Sudanese translator whispering in my ear: "They don't speak English. You must pause so I can translate your words." In my excitement, I'd forgotten that no one in the crowd could understand a word I was saying!

We slept in the same campsite a second night before flying out of the country. A huge tree towered near the spot where we'd pitched our tents, and after we'd returned from the repatriation of the slaves, Sharpton and I stood beneath this tree talking about the experience we'd just been through and the huge emotional impact it had had on both of us.

At one point, Sharpton said something about considering another bid for political office. I assumed he was talking about running for mayor of New York, as he had several years earlier. "If you run for mayor, I'm with you," I told him. But Sharpton shook his head.

"No," he said, "if I have the fire in my belly to run for anything,

I'll run for President." It took me an instant to realize he meant President of the United States. It was the first time I'd ever heard him speak about it, but I could tell he was dead serious.

"Just let me know what I can do," I replied. "I'll help you in any way I can."

Sharpton and I had gone to Sudan because Sharpton felt it was important to try and shine a light on what was going on over there. Although the slavery problem had been going on for almost two decades, it had recently gained more attention in the U.S., thanks in part to an increased focus on the issue by evangelical Christians such as Reverend Franklin Graham, the son of Reverend Billy Graham. The newly elected administration of then-President George W. Bush was also promising to address the issue, spurred on by the personal interest of Secretary of State Colin Powell.

Rev and I were hoping that our trip would help keep the slavery issue in the public spotlight. A *New York Post* reporter, Robert George, made the trip to Sudan with us, reporting back to New York readers daily about everything our group saw. His series of articles were powerful and moving, and got considerable attention back home.

As our group was about to depart from our campsite in Sudan to return to America, the leader of the village presented me with a carved wooden walking stick. "I give you this to remember—so you do not forget the suffering of our people," he said. Today I keep that stick in my study at home, along with other mementos of my travels. It will always hold a special significance for me as a reminder of how, even in this supposedly advanced era, man's inhumanity to man continues to cast a dark shadow across the globe.

When we arrived at Ghana, the first stop on our journey home, we learned that the campsite where we'd slept had been bombed the very next day by Sudanese government planes. We had escaped a brush with death by a matter of hours.

As soon as we returned to the U.S., we held a press conference where the Rev and I described in detail what we'd seen. There was a lot of international and New York-area media interest in our trip, and it all had to do with the fact that we'd personally witnessed slavery in action—an abuse of human rights so horrendous that a lot of people simply couldn't believe it actually existed. We could now speak from firsthand experience about the reality of what was happening to the Sudanese people. "Yes, slavery exists in the Sudan—we saw it for ourselves," Sharpton announced to the world press. He then went on to discuss possible solutions.

The question of how to stop this trade in human beings is a very tough one. One of the issues that's hotly debated is whether the practice of paying to free slaves, the way Christian Solidarity International did on our trip, actually gives the slave traffickers even more incentive to capture people in the first place. That's why we never endorsed this tactic in our post-trip debriefing.

Another thing we learned from our trip was that the Sudanese government benefits economically from the slave trade. In recent years, rich oil fields have been discovered in the areas where the abductions are taking place, and the slave raids are basically a way of clearing people off this land. The threat of being captured and forced into slavery has driven away many of the people who traditionally lived there, allowing for the unimpeded drilling for oil. By the time we made our trip, an estimated four million Sudanese had fled their homes as a result of the violence.

At the press conference on our return, Sharpton addressed this oil issue head on, announcing a proposal to place sanctions on any oil company that did business with the Sudanese government. "It's time for us to take the profit out of the [slave] trade," he told the assembled media.

A Last-Minute Plane Flight

Around this same time, Sharpton was making plans to join a number of New York City politicians who were flying down to Vieques—a small island that's part of the U.S. territory of Puerto Rico—to protest the U.S. Navy's continuing use of the island as a practice bombing range for their planes. Since the protest would involve trespassing on Navy property, it was a foregone conclusion that the protestors would be arrested.

Like Sudan, Vieques was another long-standing issue that had begun heating up of late. The Navy had been dropping bombs on the eastern end of the 3,300-acre island for 60 years; but in 1999, when two bombs went of course, killing a Puerto Rican security guard and wounding four others, resentment among the island's 9,000-plus residents over the years of bombs falling in their back-yard began to crystallize. Soon other Puerto Ricans, both in Puerto Rico and in the U.S., started to take up the cause as well. In 2000, nearly 500 people were arrested for participating in protests that were deemed illegal by the authorities because they involved tres-passing on Navy land. The spring of 2001 had brought a new wave of similar demonstrations.

The fact that a number of prominent New York leaders were involved in the protests wasn't surprising: Around one million vot-ers of Puerto Rican descent lived in New York City, and most of them had a keen interest in getting the Navy out of Vieques. The city was also in the midst of a mayoral campaign to see who would succeed Rudy Giuliani, and Vieques had evolved into a key issue. Even New York's Republican governor, George Pataki—who was up for reelection the following year—had embraced the islanders' cause. During the time Sharpton and I were in Sudan, Pataki had actually traveled to Puerto Rico to argue the legal case against the Navy's use of Vieques.

For Rev, joining in the Vieques protest was a way of adding his voice to an important front in the struggle for Americans' civil rights. "In my mind, Vieques is really a racial profiling issue," he told me. "If it was an island populated by whites, rather than by Puerto Ricans, our country never would have tolerated the damaging health effects caused by the bombing."

On May 1, 2001, Sharpton and the others in his group—Adolfo Carrion, then a member of the New York City Council, Roberto Ramirez, then Democratic Party chairman in the Bronx, and Jose Rivera, then a New York State Assembly representative from the Bronx—climbed through a hole in the fence around Camp Garcia, as the bombing range was called, and were promptly arrested. After being arraigned, they all boarded a plane and returned home to New York.

Meanwhile, I had been busy doing some political legwork. I knew that Rev had been absolutely serious when he'd mentioned to me under that huge tree in Sudan that he was thinking of becoming a candidate for the Democratic presidential nomination. And even though it was just a few months after the 2000 presidential election, I also knew that such a run took years of planning. With this in mind, as soon as we returned to the United States I sat down and began drafting a memo on the subject, titled "Open the Door to 2004."

I finished the memo in late May, and was eager to have Rev take a look at it. When I called him, however, he told me he was too busy to talk at that moment—he'd just found out that he had to fly to Puerto Rico immediately for a court appearance regarding his recent arrest for trespassing in Vieques.

"Meet me at JFK airport," he said. "We can talk while I'm waiting for the plane."

On my way to the airport, I mulled the situation over. Something about Sharpton's trip to Puerto Rico was setting off alarm bells in my brain. "Rev is going to Vieques for a court appearance, and he doesn't have a lawyer from the States going with him," I thought. "I don't like the sound of that." On a hunch, I grabbed my cell phone, dialed the airline he was flying on and reserved a ticket on the same flight Sharpton was taking—just in case he decided he wanted me to go with him.

I got to the airport in plenty of time for our meeting. At the check-in counter, I asked Sharpton: "Rev, do you want me to go with you, just in case you need my help?"

"That's a good idea," he said, "but I seriously doubt you can get a seat—the plane is completely full."

"No problem—I already have a reservation!" I told him.

If Sharpton was surprised, he didn't show it. "Then let's go!" he smiled. "You can buy a toothbrush when we get there. We'll only be there one night. We're coming back tomorrow."

As I had so many times before, I simply replied, "I'm with you, Rev."

Sharpton's predicted one-night stay turned into an adventure—and not a pleasant one. Our plane to Puerto Rico was delayed, and we arrived there late at night. As a result, our first meeting with the

Puerto Rican attorney representing Sharpton and the others was over breakfast the next morning, just before their scheduled nine-o'clock court appearance. The lawyer told us that the judge was planning to call the case to trial that very day, and that another 25 protestors would be standing trial at the same time.

To say that we were all shocked by this news would be an understatement. Sharpton had never heard a word about a trial taking place that day. We quickly agreed over breakfast that, since no one had known this was an actual trial date, we would simply ask for an adjournment—a request I felt should be granted without any problem.

As Sharpton walked into the courthouse, the way was lined with photographers and television cameramen. I was expecting to walk in alongside Rev, but at the last minute he sent me ahead to do advance work with the other lawyers.

After everyone had arrived in the courtroom, the Puerto Rican lawyer immediately made an application to the court for an adjournment—which the judge promptly denied. I couldn't believe it! How could they move straight into a trial that none of the defendants were prepared for? At Reverend Sharpton's request, the Puerto Rican lawyer then told the judge that Sharpton had his personal lawyer there in the courtroom and asked if I might address the court.

"Denied," the judge said again.

We'd gotten yet another surprise when we arrived at the courthouse that morning: It turned out that the prosecutors in the case were actually Navy lawyers who had been deputized as U.S. attorneys for the sole purpose of prosecuting the Vieques protestors. Now the judge turned toward the military officers making up the prosecution team. "Call your first witness," he said.

As a lawyer, I found the whole situation astonishing. The idea that somebody could be called into court without ever being informed that a trial would be taking place and then tried on the spot was simply wrong.

The whole proceeding took only a few hours. Since the charge was trespassing—a misdemeanor—it was a judge-only trial, without a jury. The prosecutors called several witnesses, while the defense team for Sharpton and his companions didn't call anyone. The judge quickly found Sharpton and the others guilty, then announced that there would be a short break before sentencing in order to give the defendants a chance to address the court.

When Sharpton's turn came he told the judge, "If Martin Luther King were alive today, he would have come to Vieques and addressed this issue." He concluded his remarks by wishing the judge a "Happy Martin Luther King Day."

Next came the sentencing. Carrion, Ramirez and Rivera all got 40 days in jail. This was quite a shock, given the slap-on-the-wrist fines that had been meted out to previous protestors. Sharpton was up next. The judge looked down at his notes and said, "Reverend Sharpton, I see you have a prior conviction—" (Rev had been arrested and jailed in 1987, during a nonviolent protest over a racially-motivated killing in Howard Beach, Queens) "—so I'm sentencing you to 90 days."

I felt my heart skip a beat. Three months! It was a stunningly harsh sentence for a simple act of civil disobedience.

An immediate request was made to stay the sentence pending an appeal, in which it would be argued that the trial had been improperly rushed and that Sharpton and his co-defendants had been denied adequate representation. José Fuste, the San Juan Federal judge, promptly turned down the request. This meant that

Sharpton and the others would be taken directly into custody. The court officers then marched the four prisoners out of the courtroom in handcuffs and leg chains. As they walked out the door, Sharpton held up one manacled leg up in front of the assembled photographers to demonstrate that he was in shackles, and suggested to his co-defendants that they do the same. The result was an unforgettable photo that would make the cover of a local New York tabloid the next day.

I immediately rushed downstairs to the prisoner's visiting area, a small cubicle in the basement containing a glass partition and telephones, where Sharpton and I could speak as lawyer and client. I was still stunned by what had taken place upstairs in the courtroom, but Rev wasn't fazed in the least.

The first thing he said to me was, "They're going to regret this. It's the best thing that could have happened on this issue." He then went on to tell me exactly what points he wanted me to cover when I spoke to the press—including pointing out that the Rev had been railroaded in the trial, but also emphasizing that what really mattered was the issue of stopping the bombing in Vieques, and that we shouldn't lose sight of this all-important fact.

Fully briefed, I walked out the front door of the courtroom and found myself standing before a throng of reporters and TV cameras. As the cameras rolled and the reporters shouted questions, I couldn't help reflecting on the irony of how I'd missed being part of the photo of everyone walking into the courthouse because I had to do important legal advance work—yet now here I was, standing in front the world media, making Sharpton's case to a global audience.

After the trial, I remained in San Juan along with one of Sharpton's aides and his videographer. As Sharpton's attorney, my name was on the visitors' list at the Federal prison in nearby Guaynabo, where he was being held, and I was anxious to get there exactly when visiting hours began.

On the morning of Sharpton's first day in jail, when it was time to leave for the prison, Rev's aide was still relaxing in a Jacuzzi at our hotel. I stood there in my suit, pushing him to get dressed so that we could go.

"What's the hurry?" the aide said. "Sharpton's not going anywhere."

I left him sitting in the Jacuzzi and headed to the jail without him.

Sharpton was being kept in a special area of the prison that had been set aside for Vieques prisoners. During his couple of days there he met Ruben Barrios, the leader of Puerto Rico's national liberation movement, who was being held in the same prison wing. Meanwhile, reporters were coming down from all the major New York media outlets to cover the story. A few days after the sentencing, I got a call from a reporter I knew saying he'd heard that Sharpton was being transferred back to the States. I called the prison at once, but they refused to tell me anything—even though I was Sharpton's lawyer!

A few minutes later I got another call, this time from Rachel Noerdlinger, Sharpton's extraordinarily competent, effective and loyal director of communications. Rachel, who was in New York, told me that Sharpton's videographer, Eddie Harris, had just called *her* from an airplane. Harris was flying back home from Puerto Rico to attend his sister's wedding. By coincidence, Sharpton and the other three members of what the press was now calling "The Vieques Four" were on same plane as Harris, being escorted back to New York under the custody of Federal marshals.

I hopped on the next available flight back home. When I arrived at JFK Airport, a member of Sharpton's staff was there to meet me. She immediately walked me over to a waiting group of reporters and cameramen. Expecting this might happen, I'd prepared a statement on the plane, which I now gave to the press along with a few extemporaneous remarks. I couldn't answer their biggest question, however, which was: "Where is Sharpton being taken?"

After my impromptu press conference was finished, I made a couple of additional phone calls and finally discovered that Rev was being moved to a place called the Federal Metropolitan Detention Center in Sunset Park, Brooklyn. I knew there was a Federal jail in Manhattan, but this was the first time I'd heard of one existing in Brooklyn. Since at that time a special attorney's pass was required to enter a criminal prison facility, I immediately rushed to the court building in Manhattan where such passes were issued. When I got there, however, I was told they weren't issuing attorney passes that day. I figured the next best thing would be to go to the appellate court in Brooklyn to get a certificate stating that I was an attorney in good standing. Certificate in hand, I drove straight to the Federal detention center where, to my relief, I was able to use the certificate to get inside.

When I was finally able to sit down face to face with Sharpton, the first thing he said to me was, "Where were you? What took you so long?"

Knowing that Rev was facing the ordeal of being incarcerated for 90 days, I didn't have the heart to go through all the problems I'd run into trying to get in to see him. Instead, I promised I wouldn't be late again, and told him that I'd be there at the very start of visiting hours each and every day of his prison term—which I was.

Jailhouse Vigil

This marked the start of a three-month stretch in which I spent virtually every daylight hour at Sharpton's side. He and his three fellow protestors had a whole wing of the jail to themselves, although they were confined at night in individual 8-by-12 cells. During visitor's hours each day, from eight in the morning until eight in the evening, I met with Sharpton in a prison conference room. This allowed us to confer as lawyer and client, and also got him out of his jail cell.

It was over those three months that the Rev and I really cemented our relationship. Not only did we get to know each other well, but I also continued to learn from him as I had during the hours we spent walking side by side leading the march for justice for Abner Louima. During this period, I saw Sharpton's inner strength and witnessed just how brilliant and focused he is. At the same time, I got a firsthand look at his incredible ability to turn adversity into advantage.

Over the next few weeks, a parade of visitors joined us in the conference room to pay their respects to Sharpton. *Everyone* came to see him: Reverend Jesse Jackson, ex-New York City mayor David Dinkins, current mayoral candidate Fernando Ferrer, Kweisi Mfume, head of the NAACP at the time, New York's two U.S. senators, Hillary Clinton and Chuck Schumer (who promised to have some chicken soup delivered), and over twenty members of Congress, including the dean of the New York delegation, Charlie Rangel. Sharpton's wife, Kathy, and his teenage daughters,

Dominique and Ashley, were frequent visitors as well. In fact, in one of his earliest interviews from jail, with New York 1 television, Sharpton got rather emotional talking about how the hardest part about his sentence was the effect it was having on his wife and daughters. He also told the interviewer that his incarceration had galvanized his thoughts about running for president.

As serious as the whole matter was, these visits also had their lighter moments—particularly where Reverend Jesse Jackson was concerned. He and the Rev like to engage in what I would characterize as an ongoing, friendly battle of wits and one-upmanship. For example, prior to getting sent to jail, Sharpton and his wife Kathy had made elaborate plans to hold a gala ceremony marking the renewal of their wedding vows after 20 years of marriage. It was a very important event, especially to Kathy. Now, however, because of the Reverend's incarceration, the event was going to have to be postponed.

Kathy didn't bat an eye. "I'll stand behind my man," she said to me. "We'll just do it when he gets out."

Meanwhile, Jesse had jokingly told Kathy that he'd be more than happy to stand in for Sharpton at the ceremony. A short time later, Jackson went again to visit Sharpton at the detention center in Brooklyn.

Sharpton greeted him with the words, "Alright, let's go—we can do it in the bathroom."

"What do you mean?" asked Jackson, puzzled.

"You said you were willing to take my place," Sharpton replied, "so let's do it. We'll change clothes, and you can take my place in jail. You can do my time, and I'll go out and renew my vows."

"Don't worry—that won't be necessary," Jackson countered. "You see, I'm going to be taking your place during the vows…and during the honeymoon afterward!" It was an entertaining moment of levity between two of the quickest-witted men in America—and a welcome break in the tension.

On one occasion when Jackson visited Sharpton in jail, he ran into Abner Louima, who also happened to be visiting that day. When it came time to leave, Jackson, Louima and I walked out of the prison together. Glancing over at the bank of television cameras that had been set up across the street from the detention center, I asked Reverend Jackson if he wanted to speak to the press. At first he replied, "I don't think so." Then, a moment later, having obviously reconsidered the matter, he walked over to the cameras with Louima and me trailing behind him.

After Jackson was done addressing the press, Abner and I escorted him to his car. We then turned around and headed back toward the cameras so that Abner could say something as well. Suddenly, we heard a screeching of brakes. It was Jackson, motioning for us to come over. He leaned out of the car window and said to us, "The message of my statement was very important—I don't think it would be a good idea to dilute it by having another speaker follow me."

Abner, however, being his own man, was not deterred. As Jackson drove off, we turned and looked at each other, then marched straight over to the microphones so Abner could make his statement.

Another morning, while Sharpton was still in prison, I was awoken by a frantic phone call from his wife. "The Reverend needs to see you immediately," she said. "He has something important to talk to you about."

I grabbed a copy of the *New York Daily News* before heading out to Brooklyn. On page three was the headline: "SHARPTON

ACCUSES JESSE OF SMEARING HIMSELF WITH KING'S BLOOD." I knew it was going to be a long day.

What had happened was this: The previous day, Rev had done a television interview with Fox News in which he told the interviewer, on camera, that he was worried about the risk that the media might try to discredit him—"in much the same way," he added, "that they tried to claim that Jesse Jackson smeared himself with Martin Luther King's blood after King was shot."

The night of the interview, a brief film clip surfaced on television containing only the *last* part of Sharpton's comments, making it sound as if Sharpton himself was accusing Jackson of this act. Of course, that's not what had happened—but now all hell was breaking loose.

At Sharpton's request, I quickly arranged to hold a press conference that afternoon where I read a letter from Sharpton in which he made it clear that he had never accused Jackson of such a thing. I also agreed to go on the Fox cable show *Hannity & Colmes* that evening to state Sharpton's case on the air. The show is supposed to be one of those "left versus right" broadcasts, where one host, Colmes, takes the liberal side of an issue and the other, Hannity, takes the conservative side. But on this night, to my surprise, I was getting attacked from *both* sides. They kept showing the same short clip of Sharpton, and I kept telling them that they had taken his statement out of context.

"Why don't you show the American public the whole interview?" I kept urging. "Show the full tape." Yet they never did. The whole experience taught me an important lesson about how, at times, the media can distort things by taking them out of context simply for the sake of creating controversy. Still, I was at least able to get the word out to the public that Sharpton's comment was actually a snippet of a longer statement that had been edited to alter the meaning.

Although other high-profile protestors such as Robert Kennedy, Jr., and New York labor leader Dennis Rivera also ended up serving time in prison that summer for trespassing on the Vieques bombing range, it was the jailing of Reverend Sharpton that captured the public's attention. The spectacle of Sharpton, a nationally-known civil rights activist, together with three of New York's leading Puerto Rican politicians, all sitting in prison for standing up against the U.S. Navy on behalf of ordinary citizens, seemed to sum up the nature of the Vieques controversy perfectly. The issue continued to get bigger by the day, as other Hispanics across the nation began to embrace the Puerto Ricans' cause.

A week into his jail term, Sharpton granted his first interview to the press. He used the occasion to announce that he and his three companions would be going on a liquids-only hunger strike for as long as all four were incarcerated. Some in the press suggested this was a media stunt, but I knew that Rev was dead serious. For the next month, he and the other members of the Vieques Four subsisted on nothing but vitamins, coffee and tea, and lots of water. In case anyone had doubted Sharpton was really fasting, by the end of the second week he had dropped a noticeable amount of weight—and grown a beard for good measure.

The announcement of the fast brought even more media coverage. In mid-June, two weeks into the hunger strike, the *New York Times* ran a profile of Sharpton's life in prison under the headline, "Sharpton, Sleeker by 14 Pounds, Fights On":

The Rev. Al Sharpton, somewhat trimmer after fasting for two weeks in a Brooklyn jail cell, has kept himself busy behind bars.

Every day, he said, he rises at 5:30 A.M. in the Metropolitan Detention Center and reads the Bible. He gets some exercise by walking around the prison ward 100 times or so. He showers, then meets with his lawyers or reporters or his relatives, who are allowed to visit him three times a week. He studies, receives politicians, thinks of running for office himself and shoots some hoops on the prison basketball court.

He also writes letters—most recently one to President Bush. The letter, dictated to his lawyer and handed to a reporter yesterday during an interview at the jail, urged an end to the very thing that led him to prison to begin with: the United States Navy bombing exercises on the Puerto Rican island of Vieques.

"Mr. President, you speak of compassion," read the four-page letter, which Mr. Sharpton said was faxed to the White House yesterday afternoon. "I didn't believe you when you said you wanted to be compassionate. Please prove me wrong. Show compassion for the children of Vieques. Stop the bombing."

The article also reported that, following his release in mid-August, Sharpton would be launching a committee to explore a run for the presidency.

Three days after the *Times* article appeared, President Bush made an official statement announcing that the Navy would stop all military exercises on Vieques in two years' time. Sharpton and his fellow protestors had won! While Bush's decision clearly had to do with a number of factors, including growing political pressure from the nation's Latino population to stop the bombing, I firmly believe it was the widespread media attention that Reverend Sharpton brought to the issue that finally tipped the balance in the Bush administration's calculations, and resulted in an end to the Navy's use of Vieques as a bombing range.

The same day that President Bush made his announcement, the First Circuit Court of Appeals in Boston—which, improbable as it might seem geographically, has jurisdiction over Puerto Rico—announced that it was denying the Vieques Four's appeal of their trespassing convictions. Harvard professor Charles Ogletree had presented Sharpton's case to the court, arguing that the four didn't have adequate legal representation due to the hastily convened trial, and that the sentences were also unreasonably harsh.

Losing the appeal didn't upset Sharpton in the least. From Day One, he'd been mentally prepared to serve the full 90 days. After the denial was made public, I went to the press with a statement from Rev, noting how the courts were once again being used as a tool to "politically stifle dissent and silence protest."

When I spoke to the press during this period, I never had to look far to find them. Following the start of the hunger strike, the street in front of the prison had turned into an ad hoc media center, filled with press trucks that had taken up residence. I started showing up regularly at six o'clock each morning to give the television crews an update on Reverend Sharpton's physical condition. With an entire cell block to themselves, Sharpton and the other members of the Vieques Four had a number of televisions at their disposal, all tuned to different networks. They were in the habit of turning on the local news as soon as they woke up, and so they invariably caught these dawn television appearances. "That's what we do—get up and watch you on TV," the Rev told me. One morning, he informed me that they'd seen me on every channel at once!

Every couple of days, it seemed, something new happened to stir media interest, including a letter to Rev from Coretta Scott King, Martin Luther King's widow, praising Sharpton's courage, and a statement from Sharpton's worried mother, saying that she wished she could bring her son some solid food to eat, but adding, "I feel like he's doing what the Lord wants him to do."

At the end of June, Sharpton's three fellow prisoners were released from the Federal detention center. This ended Sharpton's fast, with the Rev having lost 30 pounds in the process. As Rachel Noerdlinger, Sharpton's communications director, and I explained to the media, he had always intended to fast only for as long as the other members of the Vieques Four were in jail.

As I noted earlier, Sharpton's fasting was just one aspect of the profound personal journey he undertook during his three months in prison. Now, alone in his prison wing, Sharpton began using this time to read the writings of Nelson Mandela, Mahatma Ghandi, and other leaders in the struggle for human rights. It was during this period that I truly got to see Sharpton's inner strength.

Meanwhile, Sharpton's supporters erected a tent city across from the detention center and conducted a vigil, which included daily demonstrations. One woman, Cynthia Davis, lived in a pup tent in front of the prison for the entire last 50 days of Sharpton's sentence. During this time she suffered a number of indignities, including being exposed to a flood of raw sewage that was flushed into the street one night by a truck of unknown origin.

The politics of Vieques continued to play out, as well. Despite President Bush's announcement, many people were unhappy that it would take two full years before the bombing was stopped completely. This dissatisfaction was compounded by the fact that the judge in Puerto Rico was still handing out harsh sentences—including 30 days each to Dennis Rivera and Robert Kennedy, Jr. (who had none other than ex-New York governor Mario Cuomo as his defense lawyer), and 10 days to Jesse Jackson's wife Jacqueline, who had refused on principle to put up the $3,000 in bail money stipulated by the judge.

In late July, the residents of Vieques held a referendum in which they voted over two to one in favor of immediate cessation of all Navy activities on the island. If President Bush thought his decision was going to result in a political boost for his administration, he had clearly miscalculated.

Sharpton continued to receive a steady stream of visitors that included the various New York City Democratic mayoral candidates. The four leading Democratic candidates, Fernando Ferrer, Mark Green, Alan Hevesi, and Peter Vallone, had all publicly slammed the judge for the sentences meted out to Sharpton and his companions. Ferrer—who at one point had considered joining the Vieques Four in their act of civil disobedience on the island—was particularly vocal, calling the sentences "extreme, excessive and outrageous." Sharpton met with everyone and listened to what they had to say, but held off from backing any one candidate.

On August 15, 2001, Sharpton was finally released, noticeably thinner and sporting a full beard. He'd hoped to walk out through the front prison doors, but the prison authorities insisted that he follow standard procedure, which called for him to be driven out of the prison from a side exit in a vehicle. I joined him in an SUV, and we rode out together through the side prison doors into the waiting media throng. I'd never seen so many cameras and reporters in my life.

Once outside, Sharpton got out of the car and made his way

to a speaker's platform that had been set up for the occasion. From there he addressed the assembled crowd, which included Congressmen Charles Rangel and Gregory Meeks, former mayor David Dinkins, and Sharpton's former cellmate, Adolfo Carrion. "We'll come again if we have to, to stop the bombing," Sharpton told them. "We went into this jail struggling and we're going to come out struggling."

Being the activist he is, Sharpton was also aware that a tragedy had recently occurred near the detention center, in which a drunk police officer had run over and killed four members of the same family. Once he'd concluded his remarks, he led a march with the relatives of those who had been killed from the prison to the site of the deaths, where he lay a bouquet of flowers on a makeshift memorial to the four family members.

Leaving his prison incarceration marching was, to me, appropriately fitting for Sharpton and the activist he was and continues to be. Only then did he go home to shave off his beard before heading to his favorite restaurant, Amy Ruth's in Harlem, where he celebrated his freedom with his first real meal in months.

To me, this episode proved conclusively that one person *can* make a difference. Sharpton's imprisonment for civil disobedience is what put the bombing of Vieques back on the front page. If not for the uproar over Rev's lengthy jail sentence and the renewed interest it engendered in Vieques, I believe the U.S. government would not have addressed the issue at that time. Thanks to Sharpton, Vieques became a huge story all over the country, causing people who hadn't known anything about the issue to suddenly begin focusing on it, which in turn forced the government to respond.

Sharpton felt his overly harsh sentence from the judge in San

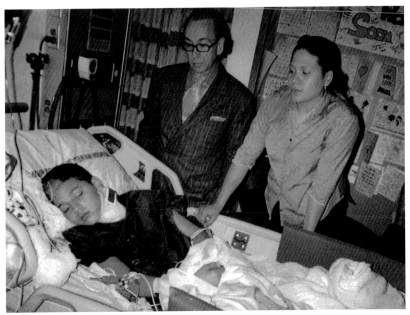

Standing at the bedside of Angel Reyes with his mother, Diana Reyes, at Cornell Weill Medical Center.

Speaking at a press conference in front of the Queens Courthouse, flanked by the mothers of Vasean Alleyne and Angel Reyes, after an appearance by defendant John Wirta.

Testifying at a hearing in support of a tougher penalty in New York State for DWI drivers who cause death or serious injury.

Walking with Angel Reyes as he returns home after his lengthy hospitalization and rehabilitation.

Consulting with Johnnie Cochran in the early stages of the Louima case, at a Saturday rally at Reverend Al Sharpton's House of Justice in Harlem.

Addressing the press outside The Brooklyn Hospital Center, where Abner Louima was hospitalized after being attacked in a police precinct house.

Announcing the settlement of Abner Louima's civil case against the City of New York and the Police Benevolent Association. Also pictured: To my right, Abner Louima and Johnnie Cochran, and directly behind me—backing me up as always—my partner, Scott Rynecki.

In Sudan with a delegation, led by Reverend Sharpton, that was investigating modern-day slavery.

At Kennedy Airport answering questions from the press after my return from Puerto Rico, where I had accompanied Reverend Al Sharpton for his court appearance for trespass at the Vieques naval base.

With Reverend Sharpton in one of our daily jailhouse visits at the Federal Metropolitan Detention Center in Brooklyn.

Marching in front of the Federal Metropolitan Detention Center in Brooklyn during Reverend Sharpton's incarceration there.

Reverend Sharpton addressing the media upon his release from jail after serving his 90-day sentence for trespassing on the U.S. Navy's bombing range in Vieques.

Speaking to a group of protestors in front of Chelsea Mini-Storage in Manhattan, site of the shooting death of Ousmane Zongo.

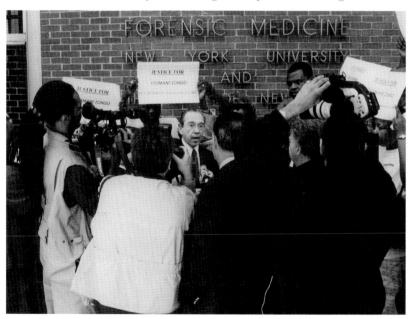

Addressing the media in front of the offices of the New York City Medical Examiner while the autopsy of Ousmane Zongo is being conducted inside.

At the Ouagadougou airport, as Ousmane Zongo's widow and his older brother view his remains for the first time upon the return of his body to Burkina Faso.

Addressing the press after the sentencing of Bryan Conroy for the killing of Ousmane Zongo.

Juan was the tipping point in the Vieques situation. "Martin Luther King always said that they never would have won the Battle of Birmingham without a Bull Connor on the other side," he told me. "That judge was our Bull Connor."

I also think that the 90 days Sharpton spent in jail over Vieques crystallized his position as a civil rights leader in the American public's mind. After all, Vieques was a Hispanic cause, not an African-American one—and yet Rev brought to it the same passion and commitment that he's brought to black civil rights issues.

For me, those three months were an opportunity to witness firsthand one of our country's great civil rights activists in action, as well as a chance to really get to know Sharpton the person. Today, I keep a photo on my office wall of the Rev in his prison garb, taken just before his release from the Metropolitan Detention Center. The inscription reads: "To my friend and brother Sandy. We did it together. Thanks. Peace. Rev. Al Sharpton, 8-16-01, MDC."

CHAPTER FIVE

JUSTICE FOR ZONGO!

A Shooting in Chelsea

IT WAS 9:00 A.M. on December 9, 2005, and a cold wind was sweeping across lower Manhattan. An early snowstorm had dumped five inches of wet, heavy snow on New York City the night before, and the downtown traffic was unusually light for a Friday morning. The one exception was the space immediately outside the 20-story municipal courthouse on 111 Centre Street, where a dozen cameramen and reporters from the television networks had set up camp on the small concrete plaza. They were there for the same reason I was: Today was the day when Bryan Conroy, until very recently an officer in the New York Police Department, would be sentenced for the killing of an innocent, unarmed man named Ousmane Zongo in the course of a police operation that went terribly wrong.

I knew many of the reporters by name, but I wasn't interested in talking to them right now—there would be time for that later, at the sidewalk press conference following the sentencing. In my heavy overcoat, I was oblivious to the cold. My only thoughts were about the clock. I was waiting for Ousmane's uncle, Adama Somkeita Zongo, who had been delayed by the snow. Adama, like his nephew, was a native of Burkina Faso, a small nation in West Africa. His nephew Ousmane had joined him in New York City in 2001 to earn money repairing imported African artifacts, which were often chipped or broken in transit. The money the younger Zongo had been making not only supported his wife and two young children back home in Burkina Faso, but also provided books for the children, medicine for the elderly, and food for the poor of his small village.

In May of 2003, just weeks before he was scheduled to return home for good, Zongo's dream of a better life for his family and neighbors ended abruptly in the corridor of a Manhattan storage facility at the hand of Officer Conroy. It was a tragic case of being in the wrong place at the wrong time: Conroy, a young, relatively inexperienced cop, was working in plain clothes that day. He'd been left to stand guard on a locker of illegal CDs, following a raid by his team on a CD-counterfeiting ring that had been operating out of the warehouse.

Zongo, who used a nearby storage space as his workshop, came out into the hallway and saw a man dressed in street clothes holding a gun in his hand—Conroy. Exactly what happened next would be the subject of a lengthy investigation and many hours of conflicting court testimony, but the final result was all too clear: Zongo lay fatally shot in the hallway of Chelsea Mini-Storage with four bullet wounds to his abdomen, chest, arm and upper back.

The shooting made the front page of the *New York Times*, where I'm sure many Americans read the news with a regretful shake of their heads over the sad death of this husband and father, so far from his home. But for the West African community of New York City—and for people of color, in general—Zongo's death represented something greater than simply one more random tragedy in the big city. It was yet another chilling reminder of how they're all at risk of becoming the victim of an overeager policeman's gun whenever they step out their front door.

That stark reality was the reason I was standing on the snowy sidewalks of downtown Manhattan this December morning. As with the Abner Louima case, I was once again on the front lines of the civil rights movement against excessive use of force by police—this time with my colleague, Michael Hardy, as co-counsel—representing the Zongo family as they attempted to get justice for their relative's wrongful killing.

I never met Ousmane Zongo when he was alive, but in death I had come to know him well. He was an honorable man, and he didn't deserve to die the way he did. As an attorney representing his family, an important part of my responsibility was to work within our justice system to see to it that the city of New York and the New York Police Department were held accountable for Zongo's death. This was crucial for two reasons: First, Zongo's family deserved to see justice done for what happened to him. In addition, holding the police accountable both criminally and civilly—where appropriate—in police shootings like the one that killed Zongo is, I believe, an essential step toward preventing such shootings in the future.

Today marked the end of the first phase of this fight for justice: the criminal trial of Bryan Conroy. Actually, it was Conroy's second criminal trial. The first had ended in March of 2005 in a deadlocked jury (according to press reports, the final vote had been 10 to 2 for conviction). The second trial's biggest moment had come two months earlier, when Conroy was found guilty of criminally negligent homicide by the presiding judge, following a non-jury bench trial. From a civil rights standpoint, Conroy's conviction was extremely significant: It was one of the very few times in U.S. history that a white police officer had been convicted for shooting a black man in the course of a police action. The judge's guilty verdict sent a message to police everywhere that they can and will be held accountable for unwarranted shootings.

The guilty verdict also meant that Zongo was cleared of any wrongful behavior in the moments leading up to his shooting. "Now I can tell my sons that their father was a good man, and was not to blame for his death," said Zongo's widow, Salimata Sanfo, after the verdict was announced.

In a way, today's sentencing was something of an anti-climax. Compared to Conroy's all-important homicide conviction, the sentence itself was much less significant. At most Conroy was facing five years in jail, and in all likelihood he would serve a lot less time than that, if he went to jail at all.

Nine-thirty, and Zongo's uncle was still nowhere in sight. I'd wanted him in court to read a statement from Zongo's widow to the judge before the judge passed sentence. Now it looked like I'd have to ask someone else to read it—probably one of the leaders of the local West African community.

Meanwhile, since I had no way of knowing what the sentence would be, I was carrying two different press statements of my own, for when I met with the media later. In my left breast pocket was the statement I would make if Conroy was sentenced to jail. In my right pocket was what I would say if Conroy got no jail time. You can never predict what a judge might do: He could decide to make an example out of Conroy and throw the book at him, or he could place the lion's share of the blame on the NYPD, based on the voluminous testimony about the shoddy manner in which the police department had handled the raid, and let him off with probation.

I made my way through the courthouse entrance reserved for police, court staff and attorneys, and rode the elevator to the twelfth floor. By now I'd spent so much time in room 1234, the courtroom where the trial was being held, that it felt like a home away from home. I chatted briefly with Shirley and Andrea Shepard—the mother-daughter team of sketch artists that can be seen at every high-profile trial in New York, sitting upfront with their chalk and drawing paper—as I kept one eye on the print and TV reporters filling up the two front rows of seats in the jury box, now being used as a gallery.

Finally, I followed everyone else in and settled into the last row on the left side of the courtroom, next the leaders of the West African community. The seating was just like at a wedding: On the right side of the center aisle sat Conroy's supporters, including his wife and relatives, a number of police officers dressed in street clothes, and other friends. On the left side of the aisle were a number of men and women from New York's West African community, some members of the court patrol from Reverend Al Sharpton's National Action Network, my co-counsel Michael Hardy, and myself. All but one person on Conroy's side of the courtroom was white, while I was the only white person on our side of the courtroom.

The courtroom was nearly full when Steve Dunleavy, the veteran (and very conservative) *New York Post* columnist, wandered in dressed in a black leather jacket. Dunleavy is a big police supporter, and he and I usually find ourselves on opposite sides of the fence, but he'd recently become interested in one of the cases I was currently working on—a case involving human body tissues that were illegally harvested from corpses without consent of the dead people's families—so I walked over to have a quick word with him about it.

Ten o'clock drifted into 10:30, then 10:45. The judge was late in taking the bench, which was unusual for him. Meanwhile, the two press statements were burning holes in my suit jacket. *Which would it be?* I wondered. *Left pocket or right? Jail or no jail?*

On the afternoon of May 22, 2003, Ousmane Zongo, a 35-year-old woodworker of African descent, was shot four times at his place of business on the third floor of Chelsea Mini-Storage, a large self-storage facility that takes up an entire city block between West 27th and West 28th Street in Manhattan. He died a few hours later at nearby St. Vincent's Hospital.

Chelsea Mini-Storage is not a warehouse that just anyone can wander into. To gain access to the upper floors, you first have to get a pass at the first floor security booth, then be escorted to your floor by an elevator attendant. Many African entrepreneurs who deal in African crafts and furniture rent lockers in this warehouse to store their merchandise; the first floor is also an unofficial marketplace for their goods. If one of their pieces became cracked or broken during shipping, Zongo was the man they went to to get it repaired. He'd been working in New York City for two years, and had finally made enough money to start his own import-export business. He was planning to fly home in June to be reunited permanently with his wife and two young children.

The person who shot and killed Zongo was a young police officer named Bryan Conroy. Conroy, a three-year veteran, was part of a plainclothes unit called the Staten Island Task Force. That Thursday, a half-dozen officers from the task force had traveled from Staten Island to Manhattan to make a bust on a counterfeit CD ring operating out of the Chelsea warehouse. They burst in on the sixth-floor headquarters of the operation and arrested one of its members. After encountering another suspect in the elevator and arresting him as well, the police then moved to the third floor—the same floor where Ousmane Zongo had his rental unit—to locate and secure a locker where some of the bootleg compact discs were stored. Conroy was left there to guard the locker.

Zongo, meanwhile, had been working in his own storage locker nearby. Apparently, he heard the commotion and went out into the hallway to see what was going on. According to one witness's account, he saw Conroy in the hall, dressed in street clothes and brandishing a gun. Apparently thinking he was about to be robbed, Zongo panicked and ran several hundred feet through the maze of corridors until he reached a dead end. At that point I believe that Conroy, who had been chasing him, fired five times, with four of the bullets hitting Zongo. After Conroy's colleagues arrived on the scene, Zongo eventually was taken by ambulance to St. Vincent's Hospital. He died on the operating table several hours later—probably without ever knowing that the man who shot him was actually a police officer.

At the time Zongo was killed, I was in Cuba with a group from Manhattan's 92nd Street Y. Although there was an embargo restricting Americans from spending money in Cuba, my group had been granted a special license by the U.S. Treasury Department to participate in a religious mission to Cuba. The purpose of our

trip was to demonstrate solidarity with the Jews of Cuba by praying with them in their synagogues, visiting their cemeteries, and
generally showing support for the continued practice of Judaism
under the regime of Fidel Castro. It had been a fascinating visit: As
a fan of vintage automobiles, I was especially struck by the 1950s-
era cars that filled the streets. The cars, all holdovers from pre-
revolutionary Cuba, had been reconditioned to run superbly, and
the sight of them took me back to my adolescence.

Watching television as I worked out in the gym at my hotel
in Havana one night, I saw a story on CNN about two innocent
people who had both died that week under questionable circumstances in police-related incidents in New York City. One of them
was Alberta Spruill, a city employee who'd suffered a fatal heart
attack when the NYPD, searching for a reported drug dealer, mistakenly raided her apartment. At six in the morning, a dozen elite
police knocked down her front door with a battering ram, threw in
a stun grenade, then arrested and handcuffed the terrified 57-year-
old woman, who promptly went into cardiac arrest and died.

The other report was about the death of an unarmed African
in Chelsea who, while going about his business in a self-storage
unit, had been shot and killed by the police. Hearing about the
incident, I immediately thought of Amadou Diallo, the African immigrant who was struck by 19 bullets when he was shot at 41 times
by New York City police while he stood unarmed in the entrance
to his apartment building. The Diallo slaying occurred in 1999,
when Rudolph Giuliani was mayor of New York City. I'd hoped
that the election in 2001 of a new mayor, Michael Bloomberg, and
his subsequent appointment of Ray Kelly as police commissioner
would bring about a long-overdue shift of mindset on the part of
the police.

That hope had been reinforced when Bloomberg showed up at Reverend Al Sharpton's Martin Luther King Day rally in early 2003—the first time a New York City mayor had ever attended the event. Surely, I thought, this meant things were changing. But now the same thing was happening all over again: In the space of a single week, through absolutely no fault of their own, two people's lives had been snuffed out by New York City police officers.

American cell phones don't work in Cuba, which was one reason I'd welcomed the trip. As much as I love the work I do as an attorney, I'd relished the chance to get away for a few days from the pressures of my New York law practice and my responsibilities helping Reverend Al Sharpton in his recently launched exploratory campaign for president. Now, though, all I could think about was getting back home and picking up where I'd left off.

I touched down at JFK airport on the evening of Sunday, May 25th, and immediately checked my voicemail. There were 22 messages, including one from Sharpton. I called him right away, and he told me he wanted to discuss the Zongo incident—tonight, if possible.

"No time like the present," I replied. It was 11:00 P.M.; I drove straight from the airport to meet with him.

Once we were face to face, Sharpton quickly brought me up to date. "We don't know all the exact facts yet," he said, "but it appears that an innocent African man has been killed by the police. I got a call a little while ago from one of the leaders of the African community in New York. Zongo's uncle has been in touch with them, and he told them he wants to meet with me to discuss what happened. I want you to be there, too."

"I'll be there," I said. "Just tell me when and where."

"We've set the meeting up for tomorrow, at my office in

Harlem. Michael Hardy has already met with some of the Africans."
Hardy, of course, was the longtime counsel for the National Action
Network, Sharpton's civil rights organization. "I'm going to rec-
ommend to the family that you and Hardy handle the matter,"
Sharpton continued. "What's important here is that we keep our
focus: Before we file any lawsuits, we have to seek justice."

I knew what Sharpton meant by this: Our first and most important priority would be to push for a criminal prosecution of the police officer who shot Zongo. Any filing of a civil action for monetary
damages would come later.

As I've learned from experience, this approach would also end
up benefiting our civil case when the time came to pursue it. A successful criminal prosecution invariably strengthens a lawyer's hand
in any civil litigation that follows. For one thing, in a subsequent
civil case a criminal conviction can serve as the basis for a successful motion for summary judgment regarding the issue of fault.
If this motion is granted, the civil case is essentially won—leaving only the dollar amount of the damages to be determined. Also,
whether or not the criminal case results in conviction, it's very likely that the criminal trial will turn up additional evidence that can
be used later to bolster my client's civil case.

That night, following my conversation with Sharpton, my mind
was racing. I knew this was going to be an important case, and one
that would require very careful handling. I also knew the obstacles
confronting us. The Diallo case had been one of the few police
shootings in New York ever to go to a criminal trial, and in that
case the jury voted to acquit all of the officers involved. Simply
bringing the officer who killed Zongo to trial would be an accom-
plishment; getting a conviction would be a landmark achievement.

I went over all of the immediate steps that would have to be taken, assuming I was asked to represent the family. Our first move would be to send a letter to New York's then-Governor Pataki, pressing for an independent prosecutor to be named to the case. Where police misconduct cases are concerned, appointing an independent prosecutor is, in my opinion, by far the best way to get justice. In my view, local district attorneys, no matter how well intentioned they may be, are handcuffed by their dependence on members of the local police force as witnesses. In the vast majority of the cases they try, these D.A.s rely on the police to stand up in court and testify for the prosecution. If a prosecuting attorney alienates the police force by aggressively pursuing police misconduct cases, it would make his or her job a lot more difficult. This built-in conflict means that the local district attorney's office may not be in a position to prosecute a police misconduct case like the Zongo shooting as aggressively as I believe they should.

In addition, we would have to have an independent autopsy done on Zongo's body as soon as possible. We also needed to track down potential witnesses. This would require hiring our own private investigators, while also reaching out to New York's West African community to get their cooperation in encouraging potential witnesses to step forward—including people whose first instinct would be to stay silent, some because of their own immigration status, others because of their general distrust of the police.

At the same time, we needed to keep alive the public outcry over what had happened to Ousmane, to keep people from forgetting about the incident over time. It's impossible to overstate the importance of what I call "the trial before the trial"—which is to say, how my clients and their cause are portrayed in the public arena in the weeks, months and years leading up to the actual trial. As a trial lawyer, I've learned *never* to underestimate the influence of public opinion. Not only does it have an inevitable, subtle effect on the jury pool—which, after all, is drawn from the public—but the sway of public opinion, while it's not supposed to, can also have an effect on the jury's deliberations during the case.

Another reason we wanted strong public opinion behind us was that it would encourage the Manhattan District Attorney's office to take action. In any police misconduct case, there's always pressure on even the most well-meaning prosecutor to let the whole matter simply fade away. We had to provide a counter-pressure, by doing whatever we could to keep the Zongo case in the public spotlight. This meant participating in a series of public demonstrations, keeping up a steady tempo of media appearances, and staying in close touch with the press to make sure they had whatever information they needed for the stories they were writing about Zongo's death.

One thing that would help keep the Zongo case alive in the public eye was the fact that it had occurred in the same week as the tragic death of Alberta Spruill. The two cases had become linked in the press, and this double assault on the public's consciousness— a woman felled by a heart attack after the police set off a stun grenade in her own apartment, and a man chased down and shot to death while working in his place of business—had amplified the community's outrage over these senseless deaths.

The Spruill family had hired Johnnie Cochran to represent them. In my opinion, they couldn't have made a better choice; as I noted in Chapter Three, Cochran was an absolutely brilliant legal tactician. With the Spruill and Zongo killings now having been linked by the media, I was looking forward to working with him once again.

The Right Man for the Job

I couldn't wait to get started on the Zongo case. Without wanting to sound egotistical, I knew I was the right man for the job. Thanks to my experience in representing Abner Louima, I understood exactly how to deal with the media in this sort of high-profile case. It also seemed a natural fit in terms of timing. The final aspects of the Louima case were just about completed, and it was the ideal moment to take up another lengthy battle to get justice while at the same time trying to effect change in law enforcement practices—which is what the Zongo case was shaping up to be. Whatever the actual details of the shooting turned out to be, one thing was glaringly obvious: His death was the tragic result of an incredibly inept and careless police action. It was up to the Manhattan District Attorney to get justice on the criminal side, and up to our own legal team to hold the city and the police department accountable for this fatal carelessness, including both monetary damages and what's known as "equitable relief," which is the legal term for non-financial concessions on the part of the defendant. In a case like the Zongo shooting, getting equitable relief for my clients might involve negotiating key changes in the way police go about their business—changes that hopefully will make such tragedies much less likely in the future.

I was also looking forward to working with Michael Hardy on the case. I'd followed and admired Hardy for years in his dual roles as counsel both to the National Action Network and to Reverend Sharpton himself. He's a first-rate lawyer, and completely dedicated to the movement for social justice. The day after I arrived back in New York, I met Hardy and Sharpton at the network's annex headquarters, where Sharpton had arranged a meeting with Ousmane Zongo's uncle, Adama, and the leaders of New York's West

African community.

I was the only white person in the room. Sharpton introduced me around. "He's a white guy, but he's okay," he told the group. The community leaders wanted to know what rights the Zongo family had regarding Ousmane's death and how they might go about seeking justice through the legal system. We explained to them that a case like this has two parts: first came the criminal investigation and (if an indictment is handed down) a criminal trial; then, after the criminal phase was completed, a civil action would be brought, in which the family would seek damages for their relative's wrongful death.

At that point, Zongo's uncle and the other leaders from the African community asked Sharpton for suggestions on who should represent the family's interests. Sharpton suggested that Hardy take on the case, and that I join him as co-counsel. Zongo's uncle and the other Africans already knew who I was: Many of them had seen me on TV during the news coverage of the Louima case. Zongo's uncle then turned to me and formally asked me if I'd agree to become involved. Naturally, I said yes.

Cases are never decided in the courtroom alone; many are actually won or lost in the preparation phase. In any case involving a shooting or similar incident, the several days immediately following the event are absolutely critical. What is done—or not done—in those first few days will have a huge impact when the civil case is finally tried, which is likely to be years down the road.

With the Zongo case, the strength of our future civil lawsuit would rest on how good our evidence was—including the quality of our experts (and their testimony). Hardy and I knew that if we wanted to win the Zongo civil case years from now, we had to get the best people on the case *today*. This meant locating a coroner to do an independent autopsy, and also procuring our own experts to examine the crime scene and the clothing that Zongo and Conroy were wearing in order to evaluate the forensic and ballistic evidence.

Of course, we could always choose to rely instead on the official autopsy and police report; but I wanted our own experts involved in the case as well—not just because they might see things differently from the city coroner or police investigators, but also because this would give us access to their expert consultation prior to trial, as well as the option of calling these same experts later as witnesses if the civil suit went to trial.

In order to focus media attention on the Zongo shooting, a demonstration had been planned for late afternoon on May 28 outside the warehouse where the shooting had taken place, on a cobblestoned stretch of West 27th Street. Since Reverend Sharpton was out of town, it was up to me and the members of Sharpton's civil rights organization, the National Action Network, to make the event significant. When I arrived at the storage facility, a group of African men were huddled in front of the entrance, milling around without any real direction or sense of what action to take: all they knew was that they were there to protest the killing of their colleague, Ousmane Zongo. Before I could start helping to organize things, one of the TV reporters covering the event asked if he could go up to the third floor and film the actual scene of the shooting. One of the most important rules in dealing with the media is to keep things interesting and informative—so I agreed on the spot.

"In fact, let's get everybody up there who wants to go," I announced. The security guard said he would take up only one group, no more; so two dozen cameramen, photographers and reporters all trooped in after him single file, heading up two flights of stairs to the maze of locker-lined corridors where the shooting took place. As we traced the zig-zag path that Zongo had taken as he was fleeing Conroy, it was apparent that he had been running for his life. Finally, we arrived at the cul de sac where the shooting had occurred. It was my first visit to the spot, and the hair rose on the back of my neck when the security guard pointed out two bullet holes in the wall. I stood by the holes as the television cameras whirred.

Once everyone had gotten their footage and photos, we all headed back downstairs to the site of the rally, where the National Action Network's crisis director and I began to fashion some order out of the chaos. The group quickly grew to 200 people, now organized into a single unit. We began marching in a slow circle up and down the street, chanting the phrase made famous by Reverend Sharpton: "What do we want? Justice! When do we want it? Now!"

Eventually, the protestors and the TV crews gathered around one of the loading docks, where various people took turns making a series of short speeches. When my time came to speak, one thought sprang clearly to mind: "The killing has got to stop!" I told the crowd. Not only did this statement focus attention on the concern that was foremost in everyone's minds, but it was also an effective sound bite—the type of statement that had an excellent chance of making it onto the evening news. As I'd hoped, my exhortation was featured prominently that night in news broadcasts of the event, thereby helping to keep the tragedy of Ousmane Zongo's killing in the media spotlight.

Our call for an independent prosecutor in the Zongo case was rebuffed almost immediately by Governor Pataki. He had his office quickly issue a statement indicating that, for the moment at least, the Governor intended to take a wait-and-see attitude toward the matter. This meant we had to shift to Plan B, which was to help convince the Manhattan District Attorney, Robert Morgenthau—a revered local prosecutor—to convene a grand jury to review the shooting. The grand jury would then determine whether there was legally sufficient evidence that the police officer who shot Zongo had committed a criminal offense to authorize a formal prosecution of the officer.

Meanwhile, there had been an important development in the case: Using our own contacts, we had uncovered a witness to the encounter between Zongo and Conroy. I arranged that same evening to give interviews with the witness to one print reporter and one television reporter.

At ten o'clock that night, after Sharpton returned from out of town, I met with him and Michael Hardy to review what had happened that day. In the middle of our meeting, I fielded a heated call from a print reporter—someone I spoke with frequently—who worked for a rival newspaper of the reporter to whom I'd given the interview with our witness. He was furious that a competitor had gotten the exclusive interview.

"How could you do this to me?" the reporter shouted. "Now my boss is pissed off!" It was a reminder that the practice of granting interviews to individual members of the media can be a double-edged sword, to be handled with extreme care—particularly since staying on good terms with the press was essential in this sort of case. The key question facing Sharpton, Hardy and myself was how to maintain media interest in the Zongo tragedy over the long run. The initial shooting had gotten a good deal of coverage, but it was important to keep the story alive in the news over the next several months, in order to cement it in the public consciousness. To do that, we needed to continue giving the press new angles to report on.

One of the most important of these angles was political. The back-to-back Spruill and Zongo incidents had stirred a deep sense of concern among New York's minority community. It's hard for white Americans to comprehend how fearful people of color are about becoming the unwitting victims of police violence. While the number of police shootings in New York City has dropped in recent years, they still occur far too often. In the year 2003, in addition to Ousmane Zongo, thirteen other people would be fatally shot by city police officers.

By coincidence, on the same day we located our witness, the *New York Times* ran two articles of interest. One was about the Spruill death, noting that the city's medical examiner had labeled the death a homicide, with quotes from Mayor Bloomberg and Commissioner Kelly admitting that the police had screwed up in raiding her apartment. The other was a short article about the Zongo case, in which Kelly was quoted as saying the shooting raised "very troubling questions."

Spruill's death had already resulted in a decision by the NYPD to suspend the use of concussion grenades during apartment raids. I couldn't help reflecting, however, that our shooting case might end up being the more significant of the two cases, coming as it did just a few years after the gunning down of Amadou Diallo by police officers—a case that received an enormous amount of coverage in the media. Like the Diallo shooting, the Zongo case appeared destined to become another important part of the movement to stop these preventable shooting deaths once and for all.

During the meeting with Sharpton, we agreed that Zongo's

shooting would be a major topic of that week's regular Saturday rally at his National Action Network headquarters, where Zongo's uncle and several leaders of New York's West African community would be featured speakers. This would be followed by a demonstration the following Monday outside the medical examiner's office while the independent autopsy of Zongo's body was being conducted inside.

That Saturday, at the National Action Network rally, I stood up and addressed the group, explaining that Dr. Joseph Cohen, the forensic pathologist I'd hired, would be flying in from California to conduct an independent autopsy on Monday morning, which would then be followed by a detailed investigation of the shooting site. I also announced that we'd be holding a press conference at nine o'clock Monday morning in front of the medical examiner's building to discuss the autopsy.

Our decision to conduct an independent autopsy had already stirred a lot of media interest; all of the daily New York newspapers and most of the local TV stations had been in touch with me about it. On June 2, the day the autopsy was scheduled to take place, I found myself wide awake at 4:30 in the morning, thinking about the importance of what was about to take place. I went to the gym for my daily early-morning workout, then met up with Dr. Cohen to go over the day's agenda. The reason I'd been forced to ask Cohen—the same pathologist who had testified in the Diallo case—to travel such a distance was that many of the well-known pathologists in the New York metropolitan area already have prior connections with local police entities, preventing them from taking on cases in which the NYPD are involved.

Outside the city medical examiner's office, I gave interviews to Channel 9 (WWOR-TV), Telemondo television, and WINS radio.

"We're here today," I told them, "because we want to find our own independent version of the truth, as to why an innocent man was killed at his place of work."

The autopsy lasted nearly five hours. While Cohen worked inside, two dozen demonstrators stood outside the building chanting "Justice for Zongo!" Camera crews from CBS, NBC, and Channel 9 were on hand to cover the event. I waited nearby, knowing the media would want to hear the autopsy results as soon as possible.

Cohen's examination confirmed that there were four bullet wounds: three that penetrated Zongo's torso, and one graze wound above the right elbow. We decided to release the findings the following morning, knowing they would set off a torrent of speculation in the press. From Cohen, I also learned for the first time that Zongo had lived through the shooting, surviving long enough to make it to St. Vincent's Hospital, where he died on the operating table. This meant that he had almost certainly endured conscious pain and suffering—a fact that would make the potential damages in his family's civil case significantly greater than if death had occurred immediately.

Later that day, our team went to the warehouse to investigate the scene of the shooting and examine Zongo's storage locker. Cohen, our forensics expert, studied the two bullet holes in the wall, as well as the location of another bullet that didn't quite make sense: It was found around the corner from where Zongo had fallen, suggesting that at least one shot might have occurred in a different place than we'd originally thought.

From there we went to the NYPD Internal Affairs Bureau, where Cohen inspected the clothing worn by Zongo and Conroy— all except one piece. For some reason, the prosecutors would not permit our inspection of the postal worker's jacket that Conroy had been wearing at the time of the shooting. The jacket was already the subject of controversy: Inexplicably, Conroy had been allowed to take it home with him after the shooting; he then waited a full five days before turning it in as evidence—an investigatory misstep that had immediately been trumpeted by the New York press. (The day before Cohen's autopsy, the *Daily News* ran an article under the headline "RIP COPS ON ZONGO EVIDENCE," in which I was quoted as saying, "An important piece of evidence has been tainted.") I'd been hoping we could check the jacket for gunpowder residue and bloodstains, which might have helped explain what happened to Zongo. The fact that we weren't allowed to examine the jacket was frustrating—but what did it mean?

The media coverage of these events was intense, as I'd known it would be. That evening, CBS ran a piece about the case on the 6:00 news called "Search For the Truth." The local cable station New York 1 also did a piece, talking about the latest developments in the case.

That night, I attended a meeting with 75 leaders from New York's African community, held in the state office building in Harlem. I had been asked to speak to the gathering, and as I stood at the podium looking out at the assembled group I realized once again what a collection of diverse people and interests New York City is made up of. Protecting every member of this diverse population was something we all had to be concerned with, I thought. I promised the group I would get justice for Zongo. The burden was now on my shoulders; it was a challenge I was more than ready to accept.

As I headed to the office the following morning, I found myself thinking about how well I'd gotten to know Abner Louima in our years of working together, and how I'd never have the same chance to know Ousmane Zongo. By this time, we'd come up with a total of three people who had witnessed the initial encounter between Zongo and Conroy. None of the three, however, had actually seen Conroy fire the shots that killed Zongo. The first witness didn't see much of anything, while the second witness said he had merely seen Zongo running down the hallway. The third witness, an elevator operator in the building, did offer one important piece of evidence: He claimed that Conroy's badge had not been visible during the incident.

The Manhattan District Attorney's office had asked us if we would bring these witnesses straight to them, rather than to the police. As unlikely as it sounds, there's always something of a competition between the police and the D.A.'s office when it comes to bringing in witnesses. After talking it over, Hardy and I agreed to deliver our witnesses, along with their respective counsel, directly to the prosecution. Since the case involved a killing by a police officer, we knew the witnesses would feel more comfortable talking to the D.A.'s detectives, as opposed to being interviewed by NYPD investigators.

The next day, operating below the radar, I arranged for an engineer to visit the site of the shooting. I was concerned about press reports saying that the lights in the warehouse hallway had been flickering—a fact that could help Conroy's side of the case, since it might help explain why he reacted the way he did. As we arrived at the hallway where Zongo was killed, however, the building representative told us that the bulbs we saw burning were the same bulbs that had been on during the shooting—none had been changed since then—and they were all clearly *not* flickering. Another important point for our side.

I had also learned that NBC was going to break a story that

evening revealing that during the raid the police never properly secured the floor with uniformed officers. This was all very important for our civil case. Each day, evidence was piling up showing that the police had been sloppy in the way they'd conducted their raid on the warehouse. Between cops not showing their badges and failing to follow proper procedure, it was looking like we'd have a good shot at proving negligence on the part of the NYPD.

Mission to Ouagadougou

At the family's request, it was agreed that Ousmane Zongo's body would be flown back to his home in Burkina Faso for burial. In 1999, Reverend Sharpton had accompanied Amadou Diallo's remains back to Guinea. Now, four years later, Sharpton had obligations related to his planned presidential run and would be unable to make a similar trip. He asked me if I would accompany Zongo's coffin to Africa in his place, and I readily agreed. The body would be leaving by plane on Saturday, June 7—and I would be going with it. The plan was that on Friday, the day before the flight, Zongo's coffin would be walked through the streets to a special memorial service at a mosque on 116th Street and Eighth Avenue in Harlem. Afterwards, the people attending the service would escort Ousmane's remains the ten blocks back to the funeral home, where it would be readied for the flight to Africa.

The service went off as planned, with a number of eloquent speakers decrying what had happened to Zongo and calling for justice. The media had requested an opportunity to take pictures of the event, and so I'd asked the mosque officials to bend their rules and allow some photographers to enter the mosque for the service. They agreed—provided the photographers removed their shoes before entering.

As it turned out, the ten-block walk from the mosque back to the funeral home grew into a full-blown public demonstration, attracting hundreds of angry marchers. The protest was a spontaneous expression of the outrage felt by many New Yorkers over yet another police killing. Coming when it did, the day before his body was to be flown home, it also put an exclamation point on the story of Zongo's tragic death. Thanks to my efforts to accommodate the media, the day's events got major coverage in the local television and print media, and were also the subject of the following Associated Press story that ran nationwide:

Ousmane Zongo's Funeral Swells into Protest of Killing
By MICHAEL WEISSENSTEIN
THE ASSOCIATED PRESS
Friday, June 6th, 2003

A West African immigrant shot dead by a plainclothes police officer was memorialized Friday at an hours-long Harlem funeral that slowly built from a solemn Muslim service into a vocal political protest.

Mourners in vibrantly colored African tunics assembled quietly outside Francisco's Funeraria, the funeral home where the body of Ousmane Zongo was prepared for burial.

...Ousmane, a recent immigrant from Burkina Faso, had been visiting a rented storage unit where he repaired African craftwork and drums. Unarmed, he was shot after a winding chase through the facility's hallways; the Manhattan district attorney's office was investigating the shooting, and it remained unclear why the chase began.

Zongo's pine coffin was loaded into the back of a hearse around noon as a small crowd of fellow immigrants chanted a call-and-response in Arabic.

"There is no God but Allah," they sang as the procession traversed 116th Street, moving from a neighborhood of bodegas hung with Puerto Rican flags to blocks of African shops and storefront mosques.

The procession arrived about an hour later at the Masjid Aqsa on Frederick Douglass Boulevard, where hundreds of West African immigrants gradually assembled for afternoon prayers.

Imam Souleimane Konate remembered Zongo as a hard-working immigrant who labored to send money back to his wife and children in Burkina Faso.

He also compared Zongo to Amadou Diallo, telling the crowd that New York's African immigrants must organize to prevent further police shootings.

"Otherwise we will always be victims," he said. "We used to fear criminals. Today we have two Africans killed by police."

...The calls for African unity made way for more strident declamations of police conduct as other imams and politicians addressed the crowd. Al-Hajj Talib Abdur-Rashid, an American Muslim imam, said official expressions of regret for the killing were insufficient.

As a crowd swollen by hundreds of afternoon worshippers made its way back to its starting point, Abdur-Rashid led what now could be called a protest in a call-and-response.

"What do we want?" he shouted. "Justice!" the crowd responded. One man held up a black wallet before the television cameras.

Zongo's body will be flown to Burkina Faso on Saturday.

Saturday, the day I was scheduled to fly to West Africa with Zongo's remains, is also the day when Reverend Sharpton's National Action Network hold their regular weekly rally. Because of a fire at Sharpton's headquarters, the rally had been a movable event lately, held in different churches from week to week. This day it took place at a church in Harlem. Sharpton told the crowd that I would be accompanying Zongo's body home to be buried.

I left the rally early to go make sure the arrangements for the removal of the body from the funeral parlor to the airport were complete. As I arrived at the funeral parlor on 125th Street, I noticed a few men in traditional West African clothing waiting out front. The body had been placed in a large room, inside a simple wooden casket. A podium had been set up and the media had placed microphones on it. Meanwhile, the TV cameramen had set up their tripods in the back of the room, waiting for Sharpton's arrival.

The imam summoned me to sit with him on the couch in the first row facing the casket. In his native language, he recited "God is great," over and over—the same phrase that had been repeated the day before, on the ten-block procession from the funeral parlor to the mosque for the funeral ceremony.

A short time later, Sharpton came to see the body off. He gave a prayer over the body, then we followed the imam and other members of the African community outside, where the casket was placed in a waiting hearse. A motorcade of cars was lined up behind the hearse, ready to begin the long drive to JFK airport, but for some reason the caravan didn't move. Thirty minutes went by, and still nothing. I began to worry: The casket holding Zongo's remains was considered cargo by the airlines, and in order to be loaded on the plane, all cargo had to be there four hours before takeoff. I had already called the airline for an extension, and I didn't want to have to ask for another one.

Finally, someone went back inside to see what was causing the delay. He came back and reported that the funeral director was waiting for his final payment before he would release the body. "This is classic New York City," I thought to myself. "Even the release of a dead man's body is contingent on payment in full."

The payment was made and at last we pulled away from the curb, complete with an NYPD escort—an ironic touch, I thought. We got to the airport, and the casket was lifted out of the hearse with a forklift and taken away. It was raining fairly hard by now, and Zongo's uncle stood in the downpour, waving goodbye to his nephew's body.

The journey took a total of almost 24 hours: seven hours on a jumbo jet to France, then a ten-hour stopover in the Paris airport followed by a six-and-a-half-hour flight to Burkina Faso. The next day, when my two traveling companions (both from New York's West African community) and I finally touched down in Ouagadougou, the capital city of Burkina Faso, we were a little weary but happy to have arrived. Our mission—to deliver his remains to his home country—was about to be accomplished.

To my surprise, the foreign minister of Burkina Faso was waiting at the airport to greet us. I explained to him that I was there as the lawyer who had been asked to represent the Zongo family, and he ushered us into an airport room reserved for dignitaries. The cool of the air-conditioned room was a welcome relief after the hot African weather. My bag was taken from my shoulder, and the foreign minister introduced us to several other officials, including the senator from Zongo's home district—an extremely accomplished woman who, I would discover, had managed to break through the cultural barriers of this male-dominated society to become an important government official. The minister then asked me to brief

the group. Using photos and other materials, I explained to them in
detail what I believed had happened in the shooting.

Formalities out of the way, all that was left was to take pos-
session of the body, which we'd been told would be brought to us
immediately after landing. Suddenly, one of my colleagues rushed
in and pulled me to one side. "The body's not here!" he whispered.
"In fact, it seems to be lost."

I couldn't believe it. Lost luggage was one thing, but how could
an airline misplace a *body*—worse still, a body that *I* was responsible for? We had no way of knowing that the body had never made
the transfer of planes in Paris. (We later found out that it was Air
France who had apparently dropped the ball, so to speak.) In fact,
I was worried that the body had flat-out vanished. Frantic phone
calls were made, and finally we were assured that the body would
be placed on a flight due to arrive in Burkina Faso the following
afternoon. This meant that everything, including the funeral and
burial, would be delayed by a day.

The wait was made easier by the fact that the hotel I was staying in was surprisingly comfortable. I was relieved, for I'd been
told—mistakenly—that the lodgings in Burkina Faso were relatively primitive and not air-conditioned. The other thing I had been
cautioned about was the likelihood of encountering civil unrest.
Both of these warnings turned out to be less than accurate: The
hotel had air conditioning and it worked fine; and I saw no sign of
political upheaval in the time I was there.

The next day, Zongo's widow, Salimata, his two brothers, his
mother, and his two young children joined me at the hotel. Later
that day, we all returned together to the airport to collect Zongo's
remains. Because of the lost-body mishap, Zongo's funeral, which
was to have taken place immediately after touching down at the

airport, had been postponed 24 hours. Hundreds of people from Zongo's home village of Yako had made the long journey to the capital to accompany his body to the traditional burial grounds outside Ouagadougou. Many of these villagers, unable to afford hotel rooms, had slept in the streets overnight. Now they all converged on the airport, where a line of police and dignitaries waited to greet the body.

The coffin appeared, pulled by a small truck. The authorities pried open the lid and asked Salimata to step forward and identify the shrouded body. Seeing her husband's dead body, her stoicism finally gave way; she broke down and sobbed hysterically, her daughter clutched in her arms. The lid was put back on the coffin and it began the hour-long journey over dirt roads to the burial grounds with a large caravan of cars, bicycles and motor scooters trailing behind.

In this age of instantaneous news, with torrents of information being carried each day to every corner of the globe by thousands of media outlets, how much room is there in our public consciousness for the fate of one ordinary man?

I was asking myself this question as I stood in the cemetery outside Ouagadougou. The late-afternoon sun cast an orange light over the hundreds of dirt mounds that surrounded us. For the people buried here, these mounds are the only signs marking their final resting place. Several hundred mourners were crowded around a freshly dug grave, listening in silence as the imam from Zongo's village said a prayer. As the Muslim culture of Burkina Faso requires, the group was made up solely of men except for the single female senator I'd met earlier, who had been permitted access to the burial site because of her prominent position. The other women attending the burial, including the wife and the mother of the dead man, were gathered a hundred yards away under the shade of an enormous tree.

I was the odd man out on this hot, dusty plain, wearing a beige, double-breasted Ralph Lauren suit and tie while everyone else was dressed in traditional African garb. Some of the men bore the scars of tribal markings on their cheeks and brows. I was also the only white face in the crowd—but that's something that, by this time, I've become very used to. Suddenly, the senator leaned toward me and whispered that the imam wanted me to speak to the assembled crowd once he'd finished. I was more than a little surprised. My mind was still racing, trying to come up with some appropriate words, when the imam stopped talking and glanced over at me. I rose and cleared my throat, looking out at the sea of expectant faces. A translator stood poised beside me, ready to repeat my words in the local language.

But what could I say about someone I'd never met—whose hand I'll never shake, and whose name I learned only after he already lay dead, felled by a New York City policeman's bullets?

During my short time in Burkina Faso, I'd learned much more about Zongo the man, and about the many ways he had been assisting his home village with the money he'd made repairing African artifacts in New York. I thought of this, and how I'd accompanied this man's body 3,000 miles to deliver him back to his family and loved ones—a good, hardworking man who, just a week ago, had met his death in a third-floor hallway in Manhattan—and the words spilled out:

"I have traveled here to return the body of Ousmane Zongo to his homeland for burial," I said. "Ousmane was an innocent victim of a police shooting in New York City, where he was working to support his family. I have come here to promise you that Ousmane's death will not be in vain. The best way for us to give meaning to his life is to seek justice for what happened to him. To prevent this tragedy from happening to someone else, those responsible for his death *must be held accountable.* I promise you I will not allow the people of New York to forget Ousmane Zongo. I will fight as hard as I can, with one goal in mind: To get justice for Zongo!"

The imam turned to face me. "Blessed are those who help the dead, and who seek justice for them," he said. "God will give you the power to find truth, and to see that justice is done."

After the service, Zongo's wife and family thanked me for accompanying the body of their loved one back to Africa, and for telling them what I knew about how he had died. I was deeply touched by their generosity of spirit toward me, the bearer of such bad news. I turned to Zongo's eldest brother, whom I'd met for the first time the day before. "What message do you want me to take back to America?" I asked him.

"Tell America that when they killed this man, they set fire to our village," he said. "And the village is still burning." It was his way of saying that losing the support Zongo had provided to their village—the books, food and medicine—had made life much harder for everyone.

The pine coffin was lowered into the grave and four men began shoveling dirt onto it, working rapidly. Every few minutes, another man stepped in to replace one of them. The furious activity of the shovels sent a cloud of dust into the air, and the floating particles took on a golden glow in the rays of the setting sun. As they worked, people milled about, chanting the same phrase in their native tongue that I'd heard in the mosque in Harlem: "God is great, God is great..."

Suddenly, I realized that the chant sounded very much like the Jewish prayer for the dead: *Yeetgadal v' yeetkadash sh'mey rabbah* ("May His great Name grow exalted and sanctified"). For a moment, I reflected on how little difference there is, in the end, between us all. Maybe Muslims and Jews would get along better if we embraced in life the same common humanity we share in death. The battle to uphold the rights of individuals, after all, is fought to protect each and every one of us. It is this ongoing fight that brought me, a white, Jewish lawyer from Brooklyn, to this distant place, standing in a Muslim cemetery in a country that I'd never heard of until a few days ago, promising to seek justice for a man cut down before his time by a policeman's bullets—a man I would never know.

Once the body was interred, we moved to a nearby tent where the imam hosted a post-burial gathering for the mourners. I then drove back to our hotel with the senator to conduct interviews with the West African media. I also attempted to get hold of some contacts in the New York press. It took an hour of phoning, but I managed to reach a few reporters that I knew and respected. I painted the scene for each of them—the setting sun, the silent crowd of men around the grave, the grieving widow. Once again, my efforts bore fruit, as the description of the burial made it into several New York newspapers.

The next day, I held a press conference that was broadcast on Burkina Faso television. During the press conference, one of the local reporters said to me, "Rubenstein sounds like a Jewish name. How can you be Jewish and helping us?"

A civil-rights slogan from the sixties flashed through my mind: If you're not part of the solution, you're part of the problem. "My religion or the color of my skin doesn't matter," I replied. "When I see an injustice, I have a responsibility to do everything I can to right it." I went on to note that Martin Luther King's personal counsel had also been a white Jewish lawyer named Stanley Levinson.

The Ouagadougou press conference was a big success. Not only did we get plenty of ink in the local newspapers, but there was international TV coverage as well. When it was finally over, the deputy foreign minister thanked me from his heart.

My brief visit had given me an up-close look at Burkina Faso's culture, and I found it interesting—particularly the way women are perceived. Traditionally, the country has had a patriarchal, male-dominated society in which women are treated as second-class citizens. Of course, there were exceptions to this rule. I was particularly impressed by the female senator from Zongo's home district. "You remind me of my own start in politics, when I was a volunteer aide to a woman who served as a New York state senator," I said to her at one point. "How did you manage to achieve such a high position in your country, despite all the obstacles?"

She smiled. "It was very hard to do," she said—and left it at that.

Paradoxically, a legendary warrior-queen is revered as an icon of strength in Burkina Faso culture. This heroic woman could be seen everywhere, including the lobby of the hotel where I was staying, which featured a large sculpture of her on horseback leading her countrymen into battle. I was struck by the contrast between this image and the realities of Burkina Faso society. Since it's my custom to bring back a piece of art from each of the faraway places I find myself in, I decided to buy a small copy of the sculpture from the hotel shop to take home with me. As I was paying for it, the shopkeeper held out another small sculpture of a woman milling grain as she carried a child on her back. Thinking he was trying to sell the piece to me, I began waving him off, saying, "One is enough"—until my translator explained that the shop owner wanted-ed to give it to me as a gesture of appreciation.

"He says it is a symbol of the strength of the women in our country," the translator added. I gratefully accepted the gift.

On Tuesday, the day I was scheduled to fly back to the U.S., I woke up to hear the sound of drums in the distance. It promised to be an interesting morning: The president of Burkina Faso was out of town, but he had asked his wife to receive my traveling companions and me before we left. Following African tradition, she greeted us first in a small welcome hut before escorting us into the palace. Once inside, I found myself admiring the many museum-quality paintings by the great masters that lined the palace walls.

"They're all reproductions, I'm afraid," laughed the president's wife. "The originals are on display in our home."

We went on to have a very pleasant meeting, during which she assured us of her government's support for our efforts to get justice for Zongo. In fact, we were told, there had already been high-level communications about the tragic incident between Burkina Faso officials and the U.S. State Department.

I was still savoring the memory of our palace visit a few hours later as I stood on what seemed like an endless line at the Air France counter, waiting to get my seat assignment. It had been an eventful visit, and I'd been treated like a visiting dignitary through-out my stay. Now, clearly, I was headed back to reality.

Tragedy's Human Face

My next challenge was to arrange for members of the Zongo family to visit the U.S., in order to put a human face on the tragedy. Getting them visas, however, proved to be anything but easy. The American consulate in Burkina Faso was worried that, once they got to the U.S., Zongo's widow, his two children and his brothers would simply stay on as illegal aliens—a worry fueled by the fact that Ousmane Zongo had overstayed his visa at the time he was killed. Zongo's relatives scoffed at the idea. "I've got three wives and 28 kids here," one brother told me. "Of course I'm coming back!"

It took the intervention of Congressman Ed Towns of Brooklyn—who had also been instrumental in securing State Department approval for Abner Louima's young daughter to emigrate from Haiti to the U.S. several years earlier—to cut through the red tape and arrange visas for Zongo's widow, Salimata, and older brother, Daouda, to travel to New York in mid-summer. When it came to Salimata's two children, however, the State Department drew the line; they were afraid that if she had her children with her, the young widow would be too tempted to remain in America. Finally, it was agreed that the children would stay in Burkina Faso and be cared for by relatives while their mother was away. Personally, I was shocked that the cold bureaucracy of our government had denied these two young kids a chance to see where their father had died. As an American, it wasn't a moment to be proud of.

There was plenty to occupy me in the weeks leading up to the relatives' visit. Reverend Sharpton was in the midst of the exploratory stage of his presidential campaign, and I was acting as a volunteer jack-of-all-trades in his effort. In mid-July, there was a meeting in New York of Sharpton's brain trust, which included Dr. Cornel West, the well-known professor and author (who had just left Harvard University for Princeton following an unpleasant encounter with Harvard's newly appointed president, Lawrence Summers); Reverend Albert Sampson, a former aide of Martin Luther King; and Akbar Muhammad, who had accompanied Reverend Jesse Jackson to Syria in 1983 to secure the release of Lieutenant Robert Goodman, the captured U.S. naval pilot.

Among the items on the agenda was the civil war in Liberia, which was then at its height. The group agreed it would be a good idea for Sharpton to travel to Ghana, where the leaders of the various warring factions had gathered for discussions, to try and broker a ceasefire. It was also agreed that West, Sampson, Muhammad and I would go with him—and so I found myself flying back across the Atlantic to Africa for the second time in two months.

Despite spending days in intensive negotiations with the different groups, Sharpton's peace-making efforts were ultimately unsuccessful. Still, his presence in Ghana helped keep the story of the Liberia conflict in the international media spotlight. With the negotiations over, we had one last stop to make: The day before flying back to New York, our group spent an incredibly moving half-day at the Cape Coast Castle—the final departure point for African slaves being taken by ship to the New World. We started by taking a tour of the place, during which the guide explained how slaves had been routinely packed into the fortress like sardines—so tightly that many ended up dying. You could still see their scratch marks on the dungeon stones. Later, we stood in a circle and joined hands and sang "We Shall Overcome." Cornel West and Reverend Sampson had tears streaming down their faces, and Reverend Sharpton had tears in his eyes as well. Then we all lit candles. "Each of us has to name someone who isn't with us any-more," said Sharpton.

When my turn came, I named my mother and father, both of who had passed away some years before. As I did, I looked down at my candle and saw to my astonishment that it had a double wick—something I hadn't noticed before—with two separate flames burning. A chill ran down my spine. At that moment, I felt the spirits of my dead parents there in the room with me.

We exited the castle through the Door of No Return—the door through which so many hundreds of thousands of Africans had passed on their way to a life of slavery. As I walked through the door, I was reminded of the many difficult social problems that still have to be overcome in our own country. There had been the centuries-long fight to end slavery, followed by the fight to outlaw segregation. Today, the battle is over police brutality, racial profil-ing, and economic empowerment. The specific issues may change, but the struggle continues.

Back in New York, I began planning for the arrival of Salimata and Daouda. The timing of their visit couldn't have been better: A little more than two months had passed since Zongo was killed, and the initial media coverage of the tragedy had subsided. We had to find a way to continue maintaining public pressure for justice in the case, so that Morgenthau's office would do the right thing and con-vene a grand jury. That meant keeping the story alive in the media. Now, with the arrival in New York of Zongo's 27-year-old widow—who was leaving her children behind and journeying across the ocean from her small African village to visit the site where her hus-band was killed—the press had a new and very compelling angle to report on. The fact that the visit would occur in early August, normally a slow time for news, didn't hurt either. I knew the New York media outlets would be interested in the story once they became aware of it—and it was my job to make sure they did.

One of the advantages of being represented by an attorney like myself, who has handled a substantial number of high-profile cases, is that I've been able to develop relationships with the actual people who write the articles for the local newspapers and who decide which stories get featured in the local TV news. My first move, as always, was to fax a release to the Associated Press daybook about the press conference we were holding to mark Salimata and Daouda's arrival. The AP daybook is the first thing all the media people look at each morning when they're deciding what to cover that day; this would give them an opportunity to attend the press conference if they wished. After I faxed over the release, I followed up with a phone call to make sure the event got into the daybook.

Next, I began calling reporters I know—not just at the *New York Times,* the *Daily News,* the *New York Post* and *Newsday,* but also at newspapers that reach special segments of the public, like the *Amsterdam News,* which is the paper of record in New York's African-American community, and the *Brooklyn Daily Eagle,* which is the paper that all the Brooklyn court-watchers read. In each case, I gave them what I felt was the gist of the story, along with Salimata and Daouda's schedule for the upcoming week. I also faxed press releases to the local TV news departments, as well as to the national cable stations CNN, Fox, and MSNBC, and the various local morning shows and radio stations—in short, everyone I could think of who might be interested in the story. I then followed up each fax with a personal phone call to make sure the producers had seen the release.

Since I felt it was important to get some media coverage of

the moment when Salimata and Daouda stepped off the plane, in addition to my other calls I also gave a personal heads-up about their arrival to one TV reporter and to a trusted print reporter at the *Daily News* who covers me frequently. Although tired from their journey, both relatives sat patiently for interviews with the reporters before settling into my waiting car for the drive to their hotel. The resulting article in the *Daily News* bore a headline taken from a comment made by Salimata—"Why Did You Kill My Husband?"—and included a photograph of myself with the Zongos, fresh off the plane.

Our press conference was scheduled for one o'clock the following afternoon at Sharpton's National Action Network headquarters in Harlem. As it turned out, Sharpton was unable to attend the press conference because of a scheduling conflict. Salimata spoke eloquently through an interpreter, thanking everyone "who stood for justice for my husband." But I realized that Sharpton's inability to be there had rendered the press conference much less significant than I'd hoped. Scrambling to come up with another high-profile event to add to our schedule, I asked Sharpton, upon his return to New York, if he would lead a prayer vigil at 6 P.M. that evening on the first floor of Chelsea Mini-Storage.

From our standpoint, the vigil would accomplish a couple of things: It would give Sharpton an opportunity to meet and stand with Zongo's widow, which he'd been hoping to do, and it would also demonstrate that, despite his emergence as a national leader, Sharpton was still connected with local issues like the Zongo case. His participation would also give Rev the opportunity to keep the all-important issue of police brutality in the national spotlight.

As it turned out, Sharpton was running slightly late and didn't get to the vigil until 7:00. As I was sweating out his arrival, I got a call from CNN asking if Sharpton was definitely going to be there. "If not, we won't cover the event," the producer warned, proving once again how Sharpton's involvement dramatically raises the profile of any issue.

The move worked: While the press conference got some coverage, the prayer vigil was featured on every TV news program in the city that night and in all of the New York papers the next day. The *New York Times,* for example, ran a substantial article by Shaila Dewan on page 4 of the Metro section under the headline, "Slain Immigrant's Family Here Asking Why," along with a photo of Salimata with a tear running down her cheek. *Newsday* ran a similar piece headlined "Vigil for Slain Craftsmen—Hundreds Mourn with Widow." In it, Sharpton was quoted as calling the shooting "wrong and unjustifiable."

Meanwhile, Bryan Conroy's side was also busy getting his side of the story out into the media. His official account of the shooting, which he gave to investigators during a three-hour grilling in the D.A.'s offices, was leaked to the press the day after Salimata and Daouda's arrival. According to published reports—the leak was covered by all the major newspapers and TV outlets—Conroy said that he'd mistaken Zongo for another counterfeiter and chased him down a dead end. At that point, Conroy claimed, Zongo lunged at him and tried to get his gun; Conroy, supposedly under the impression that he was fighting for his life, shot him two times. According to Conroy, the injured Zongo then lunged at him *again,* so Conroy fired twice more.

To hear Conroy tell it, he had killed Zongo in self-defense during what he perceived to be a life-or-death struggle. The only problem was, I didn't believe his story for a minute. For one thing, the forensic evidence indicated that two of Conroy's bullets had entered Zongo from behind. For another, Conroy's account didn't jibe with what we knew about Zongo's personality. He was a gentle man, everyone agreed, and not inclined to confront anyone.

This was a message that Salimata and other supporters of Zongo would be repeating consistently in the weeks and months to come. In fact, vouching for Zongo's character was a key part of our media strategy, for a simple but disturbing reason: A number of civil rights attorneys have discovered that in cases where they're representing a victim who was killed by police, there seems to be a pattern of police trying to "dirty up the victim" by casting doubt on his or her character, motives and behavior.

This had already been happening with Zongo. For example, the police swooped in and conducted a full-scale search of his apartment in the hours immediately after his death. This "raid" was clearly designed to stir up suspicions that Zongo had somehow been involved in illegal activity; it turned up no incriminating evidence whatsoever, and many in the community felt it was completely unnecessary. What's more, as the *New York Post* noted, "Critics charge the search was eerily similar to the way cops ransacked the Bronx apartment of Amadou Diallo."

The Zongos kept a low profile over the weekend. We wanted press coverage, true, but we didn't want to overdo it and oversaturate the media, either. Besides, Monday was slated to be a big day, beginning with a meeting between Salimata and Daouda and police commissioner Ray Kelly, to be held in Kelly's offices.

At the meeting, the commissioner offered his condolences to Salimata. This was a nice personal gesture, but it was also good public relations on his side—as well as a sign of how well we'd managed to keep this case in the public eye for the past three months. If we hadn't, this meeting might not be happening. Still, in my view, the fact that Commissioner Kelly did decide to reach out was a very commendable thing.

That didn't change the fact, however, that Zongo was dead from bullets fired by one of his officer's guns. As soon as they were through meeting with the police commissioner, Salimata and Daouda stepped outside to a waiting press conference where my partner, Scott Rynecki—as fine a lawyer as there is in New York—announced that we would soon be bringing a $100 million lawsuit against the city and the police department. As usual, Sharpton summed up our position concisely. In a *Times* piece titled "Sympathy, but No Specifics for Widow of Police Shooting Victim," Sharpton was quoted as saying: "We are thankful to the commissioner for seeing the family, but we also want to make it clear that condolences is the beginning. Justice is what we seek. And at this point, justice is not on the table."

Following the press conference, Salimata, Daouda and our legal team met with Manhattan District Attorney Robert Morgenthau. At the meeting, Morgenthau told us that in all likelihood he'd be convening a grand jury sometime in October or November to hear evidence regarding Zongo's shooting. This was terrific news, for it meant that a grand jury hearing was all but assured.

There were no media events scheduled for Tuesday or Wednesday, but on Wednesday afternoon I got a call from Shaila Dewan, the reporter who had been covering the relatives' visit for the *New York Times*. Dewan wanted to write an indepth profile of Salimata, and asked if she could follow us around on Thursday for the entire day. I agreed gladly.

On Thursday, four of us—Salimata, her translator, Dewan, and I—made our way through a full day of events, beginning with a prayer service at the same uptown Manhattan mosque where

Zongo's funeral had been held. Next came a somber visit to the third-floor corridor where Zongo was killed, fulfilling the most important goal of Salimata's visit: Her culture held that if someone met with a violent death, it was essential for a loved one to visit the site of that death and soothe the spirit of the departed and bring it peace; otherwise that spirit would continue to haunt the spot in restless agony for all eternity. Following this all-important stop, we drove to the offices of Congressman Towns to thank him and his staff for their help in arranging the family's visas, then concluded our day with a formal visit with representatives of New York's Burkina Faso Association, the group that had paid for Zongo's funeral and the shipping of his remains back to his home country.

As we drove from one meeting to the next, Dewan, with the translator's help, quietly and tactfully drew out Salimata, who had been silent and tearful through much of the trip. The result was an evocative and insightful description of Salimata and Daouda's visit. It ran on page one of the Metro section of the *New York Times* the next day, under the headline "Far From Africa, a Young Wife Mourns."

"Until last week," began the article, "Salimata Sanfo had never seen an ocean.... Since then she has met people she had never heard of before: the Rev. Al Sharpton, Police Commissioner Raymond W. Kelly and Representative Edolphus Towns.... She has knelt at a mosque. She has cried in front of television cameras, signed legal papers, been recognized by strangers on the street. Today, she will take an airplane trip for the second time in her life, flying back home, where the people speak a language she understands.

"Through it all, Ms. Sanfo's face has remained so solemn that the monologue in her head is almost audible. 'I have nothing in my mind,' she said, through a translator from Burkina Faso. 'I think only of how I will take care of the children, the mother and father.'"

Salimata and Daouda's visit left an indelible mark in the city's consciousness. By the time I saw them off at JFK airport on the morning of Friday, August 8, virtually everyone in the greater New York area who scanned a newspaper or watched the local news that week would have read about the visit of Zongo's wife and brother, or seen a photo or video of the sad young widow saying her last farewell to her dead husband's spirit.

As I noted earlier, I felt that Salimata's presence in New York was absolutely vital, in order to put a human face on her husband's death. On the other side, Bryan Conroy was ready and willing to tell his version of the events leading to his shooting of Ousmane Zongo—a version that essentially pinned the blame for what happened on Zongo's conduct and, by extension, his character. Since Zongo couldn't speak for himself, we had to present his side of the case—the argument that he should be home in Burkina Faso with his family right now, that he did nothing to deserve being gunned down while he innocently went about his business, and that his shooting was a criminal injustice—through the surrogate voices of his wife and brother, as they expressed the very real grief that Zongo's death had caused.

As the Zongo family's counsel, my role was to make Salimata and Daouda's story known—to bring the sorrow and sadness that they felt over the loss of their husband and brother to the full attention of the public, through the local and national media. Their story had to be compelling, of course, or the press wouldn't have covered it. Still, someone had to serve as a bridge between the media and their subject. That task fell to me.

The Wheels of Justice

In the end, of course, all of the media coverage surrounding a case only serves as a backdrop to the hearing of the actual evidence in court. In Zongo's shooting death, this evidence consisted of the testimony of Conroy and a handful of other witnesses—none of who saw the actual shooting—plus all of the forensic evidence gathered from various sources, including Zongo's autopsies, the site of the shooting, and the clothing of Zongo and Conroy.

Salimata and Daouda returned to New York in March, 2004 to retrieve the articles stored in Ousmane's locker, which had finally been unsealed by the police. Following another African custom, they wanted to return any items Zongo had been working on at the time of his death to their rightful owners.

Meanwhile, in January of that same year, there had been yet another police shooting death in New York City. This time the victim was a 19-year-old high school student named Timothy Stansbury, who had the misfortune to open a door to the roof of his Brooklyn apartment house at the same moment that uniformed officers, on a nighttime rooftop patrol, were pulling on the door from the other side. Commissioner Kelley was quoted as saying, "At this point, based on the facts we have gathered, there appears to be no justification for the shooting."

"It was the first fatal shooting of an unarmed civilian by a police officer in New York City since last May, when Ousmane Zongo, 35, an immigrant from Burkina Faso, was shot dead by an officer in a chase through the mazelike halls of a mini-storage center in Chelsea," wrote the *New York Times*. "And it confronted the Bloomberg administration with an outcry for justice, from the victim's family and community, and from some black leaders in law enforcement and city government. Unlike the Giuliani administration's initial response to the killing of the unarmed street vendor Amadou Diallo in 1999, officials yesterday were swift to acknowledge probable culpability."

We were making progress, in other words—but only up to a point. A few weeks later, a Brooklyn grand jury concluded that there was no reason to indict the officer responsible for Stansbury's fatal shooting. It was a reminder of how reluctant grand juries are to hold police officers criminally liable for shootings that occur during the "good faith" pursuit of their duty—no matter how unwarranted the shooting itself might seem to be.

The Zongo grand jury was finally convened in late April of 2004. A month and a half later, on June 9, an indictment of second-degree manslaughter was handed down against Bryan Conroy. The next day I was quoted in the *Times'* coverage of the indictment:

"Last night, Sanford A. Rubenstein, a lawyer for Mr. Zongo's family, said that they had been told of the grand jury's actions by reporters. 'They feel they've been patient, waiting for justice,' he said of the Zongo family. The charges, if true, he said, show that the 'grand jury has done justice.'"

The first criminal trial of Conroy began in February 2005, and ended in a hung jury. According to press reports, the jury at first voted 11 to 1 for conviction. Then, in the final tally before the judge declared them a hung jury, when it had become clear that no resolution was going to be reached, one juror abruptly switched sides and voted to acquit Conroy as well, making it 10 for conviction and 2 for acquittal.

As a trial lawyer, you have certain emotions you go through in every case you try. It's interesting that, as an observer in a criminal case involving a civil client, I find myself going through exactly the same emotions when the jury is out that I do in a case that I'm trying myself—excitement, nervousness, and, above all, uncertainty. In truth, you can never predict what a jury will do. You can try to read something into any questions they might ask the judge while they're deliberating, but it's like peering into a crystal ball. There's a famous lawyer's story about a civil trial in which one of the jurors came back to the judge with this pointed question: "Can you award the plaintiff *more* than they sued for?" His query immediately threw the defendant's lawyer into a panic, while the plaintiff's counsel was in a state of euphoria.

A short time later, the jury came back…and found for the defendant! Afterwards, the plaintiff's lawyer approached the juror. "Excuse me," he said, "but I can't help wondering—why did you ask that question?"

"I was just curious!" said the juror. (The answer to his question, by the way, is yes.)

When the Zongo jury came back and announced they were hopelessly deadlocked, I was disappointed, to say the least. To have come so close to a conviction and not get it was disheartening. Still, a hung jury was a thousand times better than an acquittal. Now it was up to the assistant district attorney prosecuting the case, Armand Durastanti, and his superiors to decide whether to retry Conroy or not.

My first thought was, "What do I need to do to encourage a retrial?" Fortunately, it was a question I never had to answer, since the ever-vigilant and hardworking Durastanti made very early indications that he would indeed retry the case.

At the request of the defendant's legal team, which was headed up by the very experienced and competent defense counsel Stuart London—the same attorney who represented the officer involved in the Stansbury shooting, and who has served as defense counsel in many of the high-profile criminal prosecutions involving New York City police officers—the second trial would be a "bench trial" rather than a jury trial. This meant that the judge himself would evaluate all of the evidence and deliver a verdict. Clearly, Conroy's legal team had been shaken by his near-conviction in the jury trial, and was gambling that they would fare better with the judge than with a second jury.

The defense team also asked the judge to consider the additional charge of criminally negligent homicide, which is a lesser offense than second-degree manslaughter. Again, they were gambling. By giving the judge a middle road to take, they hoped to steer him away from a conviction on the more serious second-degree manslaughter charge, which could carry a stiff jail sentence. At the same time, though, this move carried the risk that their client might be convicted on the lesser charge whereas he otherwise might have gotten off completely.

Salimata Sanfo returned to New York for both the first trial and the verdict phase of the second trial. On October 21, 2005, the judge, Robert H. Straus, announced his decision in the second trial: Bryan Conroy was acquitted of second-degree manslaughter, but found guilty of criminally negligent homicide. When the verdict was announced, Salimata turned and hugged me for the first time.

Which brings us, a month and a half later, to the snowy December morning of Conroy's sentencing. In Room 1234, Judge Straus had finally taken the bench, and statements had been made by Conroy's lawyer, by Conroy himself, by the prosecuting attorney, and by Salimata in absentia (a West African community leader read her letter aloud to the judge). Now came the moment everyone was waiting for, when the judge would speak. The courtroom fell quiet as Straus glanced down at his notes.

"It's important to understand," the judge said, "that, not just in this case, but in any case, if a defendant receives a non-jail sentence, that doesn't mean that that defendant somehow has had his actions vindicated or minimized, nor does it demean in any way the terrible result that occurred to the victim. If a defendant receives a jail sentence, that can never be the equivalent of the life that was taken, because there's no way to measure or equalize time against life."

Sounds like he's making a case for no jail time, I said to myself.

"[W]e start out with what seems to me to be a well-intentioned police officer," Straus continued, "but one who...was insufficiently trained, insufficiently supervised, and insufficiently led." The judge went on to blast the NYPD for their error-filled conduct during the raid, describing "utter confusion and lack of leadership on almost every level."

Not good as far as a prison sentence is concerned, but the judge is making the civil case, I thought.

"I think there's a lot of blame to go around in this case," the judge continued. "But again, I'm not here to assess individual blame except that of the defendant. But he's a product of his training, and he's a product of his leadership.... There was one target. The target was arrested. And yet the first thing he does when he sees Mr. Zongo is to draw his service revolver, his semiautomatic pistol, and point it at him. Is this his training? Is this what he's taught to do?...It would appear, yes."

It's all over, I thought then. *He's shifting the blame from Conroy to the police department.*

I was right: "I've given this matter a lot of thought as far as whether you should go to jail or not," the judge said at last. "I've ultimately concluded that you will not go to jail.... I think you should be placed on probation."

There it was—no jail. Right pocket. I pulled out the statement that I'd be delivering to the world in just a few minutes, and quickly read it over:

"The widow of Ousmane Zongo feels strongly that the conviction of police officer Bryan Conroy was what was most important because it demonstrated that Ousmane Zongo did nothing wrong, and was a victory because the fault for his death was clearly found to be with police officer Bryan Conroy.... While she is disappointed that he did not receive time in jail, she hopes that the conviction of police officer Conroy for criminally negligent homicide will stand as an example to police officers all over the country that if you are a police officer and you wrongly kill someone, you will be held accountable criminally.... She believes the conviction was a victory for justice."

At tense trials like this one, in order to avoid potentially ugly confrontations between opposing camps in the corridor, the court officers will allow all the spectators on the near side of the courtroom to file out first and take the elevators downstairs, waiting until the coast is completely clear before letting the spectators on the other side walk out into the hallway. This meant that Bryan Conroy's friends and family left the courtroom first, while the Zongo family's supporters—many of whom had been there every day of both trials—had to stand waiting for a good 20 minutes before the uniformed officers let them out of the room. "That's alright," joked one woman. "We're used to it."

Finally, we were allowed to leave. I walked out toward the

elevator and the television cameras and reporters waiting on the street below. We still had a civil suit to pursue in the months ahead—and, thanks to the judge's castigation of the police department's actions, our case was stronger than ever. But that lay in the future. For the moment, at least, the wait for justice was over.

In June of 2006, I was notified that a conference had been scheduled with representatives of the City of New York and the defendant Bryan Conroy to discuss a possible resolution of the Zongo family's civil case. The new Federal Courthouse on Pearl Street in Manhattan, where the conference was to be held, is a monument to the Federal government's continuing ability to build stately courthouses that are extraordinarily beautiful. I can't help wondering whether these impressive buildings aren't somehow conducive to the pursuit of justice, in and of themselves. At any rate, the first meeting was productive, if inconclusive. There were several lawyers from the city's corporation counsel there, along with me and my partner, Scott Rynecki, our co-counsel Michael Hardy, Zongo's widow and brother (who had both flown in once more from Burkina Faso to attend the conference), plus Zongo's uncle and other representatives from New York's African community.

The first conference, while unsuccessful, marked the start of serious negotiations to resolve the family's lawsuit. Another conference was quickly scheduled, and the magistrate ordered the city to have someone from the city controller's office present at this second meeting.

On the day of the second conference, I was pleased to see that the representative from the controller's office was none other than Bernie London. Bernie is a legend in New York courtroom circles: When he shows up, it's a clear sign that the city is serious about amicably resolving the case. Besides the fact that Bernie's recommendations carry a great deal of weight with the powers that be, I was also very familiar with his style of negotiating, after many late-night sessions spent hammering out the resolution of the Abner Louima case—a negotiation in which he had been one of the city's key representatives.

After greeting me, the first thing Bernie said was, "I like your tie." I was sporting a new, rather loud, multicolored Versace number. Bernie's comment called to mind my friendly competition with the late Johnnie Cochran during the Louima case negotiations, when we used to vie each day to see who could wear the most colorful and outrageous tie—Johnnie representing the West Coast, me the East Coast. I missed Johnnie: In addition to being a great lawyer he was a wonderful human being, and I'd learned a lot from working with him on a number of cases all over the country. While he was tough and hard-nosed and always ready to go to trial if necessary, Johnnie understood the value of achieving a fair and equitable settlement, especially in high-profile cases. He also possessed a remarkable ability to break the tension that often hangs over these types of negotiations. Somehow, he had a way about him that encouraged the other parties to unbend and focus on resolving the case.

When Bernie made his comment about admiring my tie, I decided to take a page from Johnnie's book and try to break whatever tension existed in the room. At the same time, as a negotiating tactic, I wanted to signal my concern that the city wasn't prepared to offer an adequate amount to settle this case. So I jokingly told Bernie, "I'm so doubtful this case will be resolved that, if we *do* settle it today, I'll give you the tie."

"Let's see what you have to say after you're indicted for bribery," the magistrate chimed in. That gave everyone a good laugh. Then the magistrate added that he'd served as commissioner of investigation in the administration of Mayor Rudy Giuliani, where he'd been responsible for investigating bribery and other misconduct among city officials.

Suddenly, the whole tie business didn't seem quite so funny. I hurriedly clarified that I was indeed joking, and had no intent of actually *giving* Bernie the tie. Still, my ploy worked: the tension had been broken, and we were able to get down to serious negotiations.

We spent a couple of hours going back and forth making offers and counteroffers, Bernie sitting on one side of the conference table flanked by the other members of his team, our team along the opposite side of the table, and the magistrate seated at the head. Finally, Bernie announced: "If the victims will accept three million dollars, I'll make the call for three."

I knew this was the best offer we were going to get, and that if anyone could get authorization from the city to pay that amount, Bernie could. So I called Zongo's widow and brother (both now back in Burkina Faso) to fill them in. Speaking through their interpreter, they told me over the phone that they respected my opinion—adding that because I'd returned Ousmane's body from New York to Burkina Faso, we had a special bond between us. I then recommended that they accept the offer, which they did.

I believe that we achieved as good a result as could have been hoped for, as far as getting closure on this tragic episode: The police officer who shot and killed Zongo had been convicted of criminally negligent homicide; the city was paying three million in damages to the family; and the widow felt satisfied that her husband's name had been cleared.

Just as important, we'd also been successful in getting the NYPD to change their policies for the better. Thanks to our aggressive attempts to keep the Zongo case in the public eye, and to the powerful message sent by both the judge's sentencing statement at Conroy's trial and the city's very large financial settlement with the Zongo family, the police were forced to take a long, hard look at the way the Chelsea Mini-Storage raid had been conducted, including the kind of training that Conroy and his fellow plainclothes officers had received beforehand. As a result, they began a serious overhaul of their entire plainclothes operation—a point noted by the *New York Times* in their article about the Zongo settlement, published the day after the agreement was reached:

> In the wake of Mr. Zongo's death, "the Police Department reinforced training for plainclothes police officers department-wide, making certain that anyone assigned in plainclothes underwent a rigorous training program before being deployed," said Paul J. Browne, the department's chief spokesman.

I strongly doubt that these changes would have been implemented without our full-court press in the media. In the future, these new policies hopefully will help prevent out-of-control plainclothes raids like that one that cost Ousmane Zongo his life—in which case, this good man will not have died in vain.

THE FIGHT CONTINUES

ALL OF THE EVENTS described in these pages represent important victories in the struggle for justice and social change. But this fight will continue as long as our society allows the least powerful among us to be abused and neglected by those in positions of power. In the course of writing this book, I was asked to represent victims in a number of new high-profile cases that illustrate just how vulnerable the average American is to various types of mistreatment, and how the justice system can serve as an important tool for fixing what's broken. Together, these cases shine a spotlight on important areas in our nation's fabric that are still badly in need of repair:

Inequality in American Health Care

In general, America's private health care system provides reasonably good medical care for those who can afford it. Unfortunately, the same can't always be said for our public health care. All too often, Americans who are less well off and have to rely on publicly-funded hospitals end up receiving substandard care.

One of the most shocking examples of this was a case that many people all over the world have become familiar with, involving the tragic death of Esmin Elizabeth Green, a 49-year-old Jamaican woman with a history of mental illness. At 5:30 A.M. on June 19, 2008, Esmin lost consciousness and fell out of the chair where she'd been sitting for the previous 24 hours in the waiting area of the psychiatric emergency room at New York City's public Kings County Hospital Center in Brooklyn.

The fact that she had to wait for that length of time to be admitted—which was a common occurrence at this particular hospital—is outrageous in itself. What happened next, however, boggles the mind: After she fell off her chair onto the waiting room floor, the entire hospital—security guards, nurses, aides and doctors—simply ignored her, letting her lie face down for a full hour as they went about their business. It wasn't until a nurse finally nudged the unresponsive woman with her foot that the staff realized something was seriously wrong and tried to revive her. By then it was too late: She was already dead from cardiac arrest.

According to a coroner's report, Esmin lost consciousness after developing a blood clot in her leg from sitting for so long. The clot broke off and lodged in her lungs, causing her to faint from lack of oxygen. At that point, her life might have been saved with timely medical care. Instead, she got less attention from the trained medical professionals at Kings County Hospital than she would have received if she'd passed out on a New York City sidewalk.

This entire travesty was recorded on a surveillance camera. When the footage of Esmin, first falling off her chair and then lying unattended for an hour on the floor of a hospital waiting room, was aired on television and the Internet, the universal reaction was one of amazed disbelief. But in fact, there had been plenty of warning that something like this might happen. The hospital's psychiatric unit—virtually the only mental health facility available to lower-income residents of Brooklyn—had been formally cited by state officials the previous summer for falsifying documents to conceal its overcrowded conditions. At the time of Esmin's death, the unit was the subject of a Federal civil lawsuit brought by the New York Civil Liberties Union and the New York State Mental Hygiene Legal Service, and of an investigation by the U.S. Department of Justice that was launched as a result of the lawsuit.

The lawsuit, charging the unit with a dangerous level of neglect, had been vigorously opposed by New York City's Health and Hospitals Corporation (HHC), which called the legal action "grossly inaccurate, irresponsible, and an affront to the dedicated and caring staff of Kings County Hospital Center." Following Esmin's death, the city's attitude abruptly changed, largely because of the huge publicity surrounding her case—especially the shocking surveillance tape, which was seen all over the world.

I was retained by Esmin Green's family, who live in Jamaica, to represent them. Tecia Harrison, the oldest of Esmin's six children and the administrator of her estate, filed a $25 million claim against the HHC, a step that helped keep the story alive in the press while also letting the public know that Esmin had come from a large, close family whose lives were all affected deeply by her loss. I made Tecia and other family members available to the New York media, which ran a number of stories describing the family's hope that their mother's death would lead to some positive changes at King's County Hospital and in the way public psychiatric care was dispensed in general.

This public pressure helped bring about a long-overdue reaction from city authorities: Within weeks, the HHC fired the psychiatric emergency department's medical director and head of security. And while the HHC made a point of listing a number of reforms that had reportedly been implemented over the previous year—reforms that clearly weren't sufficient—they also began a serious push to make substantive improvements in the way the unit operated. The U.S. Justice Department investigation continued to move forward, but with renewed intensity, while the city's Department of Investigation announced it was launching its own inquiry into Esmin Green's death. More details were emerging about how nurses and doctors had failed to follow the hospital's own protocol in terms of providing care, and had then gone on to enter false notations in their log sheets in an attempt to cover up these failures.

In February of 2009 the Justice Department concluded its investigation by issuing a 58-page report that was extremely critical of the King's County facility. Calling the unit "highly dangerous," it noted that the medical staff often failed to provide patients with proper diagnosis and treatment, that unruly patients were often left in physical restraints even after they'd calmed down, and that doctors commonly followed the risky practice of injecting patients with more than one antipsychotic medication at a time. The report also documented a number of violent incidents that occurred at the facility in the months after Esmin Green's death, including a brawl among a half-dozen patients that left one of them requiring surgery, and several cases of sexual assault. In addition, the report confirmed that the hospital staff had falsified certain details of Esmin's case.

At the same press conference where they released the details of the Federal inquiry, HHC officials unveiled their ambitious plans to upgrade the King's County mental health facilities, starting with their relocation to a new $153 million building. The HHC also announced it was adding several hundred new staff members to the psychiatric unit, and replacing the hospital police officers— who were known for routinely using physical force and handcuffs to restrain psychiatric patients—with medical staff trained in behavioral management of the mentally ill. Other changes included implementing a new, more efficient system for admitting patients, and instituting a policy of checking on patients every 15 minutes.

All of these changes represented an important shift, as the HHC finally accepted accountability for the abusive environment that had been allowed to flourish. Hopefully, these changes will ensure that no one else has to suffer the lonely death that befell Esmin Green in that King's County Hospital waiting room.

In late May of 2009, the HHC agreed to settle the family's suit for $2 million. As part of the settlement, the corporation accepted full responsibility for what had happened to their mother. In addition to providing a measure of justice for Esmin Green's family, this outcome sends a message to local governments around the country that they will be held legally responsible for the conditions in their public health facilities.

At the press conference announcing the settlement, I made a statement calling it "fair and reasonable." But I also noted that the city's Department of Investigation's inquiry into the case was ongoing. "What remains most important to this family is the criminal culpability for those responsible for what happened and those who attempted to cover it up," I told the media. "In no way does this settlement affect that investigation, and the family remains adamant in its demands that anyone who committed a criminal act with regard to the death of Esmin Green or the attempt to cover it up be prosecuted criminally to the full extent of the law."

On June 19, 2009, exactly one year after Esmin's death, the city's Department of Investigation released the results of its inquiry, which noted the systemic failures leading to the tragedy and also detailed how individual nurses and doctors misrepresented their actions during the 24 hours leading up to her death. As this is being written, the District Attorney of King's County, Charles "Joe" Hynes—a fine prosecutor, whose responsibility it is to prosecute any hospital staff members who committed criminal acts— has convened a grand jury that is now hearing evidence in the Esmin Green case.

Meanwhile, although conditions appear to be better in the new facility, problems related to neglect and inattention are still a concern. For this reason, New York City and the U.S. Department of Justice are in the process of working out a consent decree that would allow Federal authorities to monitor the Kings County psychiatric unit over the next couple of years.

The fight continues.

Lack of Security in Our Jails and Prisons

One of the most disturbing cases I've ever handled was the recent one involving 18-year-old Christopher Robinson, whose young life was violently cut short on October 18, 2008 when he was beaten to death in New York City's Rikers Island jail complex by three fellow inmates.

While officials at the city's Department of Corrections expressed shock over the killing, there had actually been plenty of advance warning that something was seriously wrong in the Robert N. Davoren Center, the part of Rikers used to house teenaged male detainees. Another teenage inmate had been beaten to death in the same facility in 2004, and a number of inmates had sustained serious injuries from beatings in the years since then. Several of these inmates sued the city and received substantial settlements. Starting in 2007, the *Village Voice* had published a series of articles charging that Rikers guards were "deputizing" certain inmates—many of them gang members—and encouraging them to use violence to intimidate the rest of the inmate population.

Following Christopher's death, I was retained by his mother, Charnel Robinson. In addition to filing a $20 million claim against the city, Charnel also spoke with a number of reporters from New York's print and TV outlets, expressing her grief over the loss of her only child and her belief that his killing had been an "inside job."

Once again, in my opinion, public pressure made a difference. The Bronx District Attorney's office immediately launched a full-scale investigation that turned up evidence confirming a conspiracy between a handful of corrections officers at the Davoren center and a group of adolescent prisoners who essentially ran the jail for the officers, meting out violence as a way of maintaining control. Apparently Christopher, who was in jail for a parole violation (he'd missed his curfew because he was working late on his job), had refused to go along with "the Program," as it was called. As punishment, he was severely punched and kicked by several other inmates. The beating fractured a rib, which in turn pierced one of his lungs, causing internal bleeding. He died from his injuries a short time later.

In February of 2009, Bronx District Attorney Robert Johnson announced the indictment of two jail guards on charges of enterprise corruption and a third on assault and conspiracy charges. Twelve inmates were also indicted, including three on charges of first-degree manslaughter for Christopher's fatal beating. The *New York Times* ran a lengthy article about the indictments in its front section accompanied by a powerful photo of Charnel weeping as I stood beside her, holding up a photo of her hugging her son when he was alive.

As a result of the publicity surrounding Christopher's death, the New York City Department of Corrections made a number of changes in the youth facility at Rikers, including adding more guards and video cameras and instituting a policy of examining inmates for signs of violence. Three months later, in an equally important development, Mayor Michael Bloomberg signed a law requiring the Department of Corrections to regularly report violent statistics among adolescents in city jails, including all slashing or stabbing incidents as well as any serious injuries that were sustained. The law was the result of months of lobbying on the part of inmate advocates, including Christopher's mother. "It makes me extremely hopeful that lives could be saved," she told a reporter from the Associated Press.

Thanks in part to Charnel Robinson's efforts, some positive change resulted from her son's violent death. Still, inmate advocates cautioned that what constitutes a "serious injury" remains open to manipulation by the authorities. "Our concern," said Nancy Ginsburg of the Legal Aid Society, "is that they are going to be able to define out the injuries that are important to know about."

The fight continues.

Violence at the Hands of Law-Enforcement Officials

I've written throughout this book about the issue of police officers misusing the powers given to them, and about the fact that people of color are particularly at risk of becoming victims of violence at the hands of law enforcement. This grim reality was underscored once again on May 18, 2007, when Fermin Arzu, a 41-year-old Honduran immigrant, was shot and killed by an NYPD patrolman who, although off-duty at the time, was acting as a police officer engaged in a police action. Arzu had been driving his van through a residential neighborhood in the Bronx at 11:30 P.M. when he veered across the road and hit two parked cars. The police officer, Rafael Lora, lived nearby. Hearing the crash, he came out of his house in civilian clothes carrying his badge and service revolver and approached the driver's side of the van, where Arzu was still sitting behind the steering wheel. A crowd had gathered around the van at this point. According to press reports, witnesses said they heard the two men yelling at each other.

These same witnesses reportedly saw Arzu, who was unarmed, reach for his glove compartment, at which point the officer fired off five bullets in less than two seconds, piercing Arzu's heart with one of them. Lora claimed that Arzu had started to drive off, dragging Lora with him—but even if this claim, which was contradicted by other witnesses, was true, the shooting went directly against New York Police Department guidelines, which stated that an officer could fire on someone in a vehicle only if that person threatened the officer with deadly force using something other than the vehicle itself.

Coming just a few months after the shooting death of Sean Bell and wounding of his two friends on the eve of Bell's wedding, Arzu's killing reinforced the perception among New York's minority communities that the police are far too ready to shoot without justification. Michael Hardy and I were asked by Arzu's daughter to represent her and her brother. We immediately began doing what we could to assist the Bronx District Attorney's office in its investigation of the case—including working to track down witnesses to the encounter. An article in the *New York Times* in August, 2007 discussed the likelihood that Lora would be called to appear before a grand jury. In it, Hardy was quoted in regard to the fact that Arzu was found to have a blood alcohol level slightly over the legal limit for driving at the time of his death. Hardy pointed out that Lora had worked traffic duty and "had plenty of experience dealing with accidents and intoxicated drivers," adding that the facts didn't indicate in any way that Arzu "ever had any ability to use deadly force."

We proceeded to file a $25 million claim against New York City, the NYPD, and Officer Lora. In December, Lora was indicted on a charge of first-degree manslaughter. In announcing the indictment, Bronx District Attorney Robert Johnson issued a statement calling the shooting "unwarranted, unjustified and therefore illegal." I was quoted in the press as saying "this is the beginning of the journey for justice for the Arzu family."

Lora waived his right to a jury trial, preferring to have the question of his guilt or innocence decided by Bronx Supreme Court Justice Margaret Clancy. In April 2009, after a lengthy trial, Justice Clancy cleared Lora of the first-degree manslaughter charge but found him guilty of second-degree manslaughter. This was a significant victory for victim's rights—since, as noted elsewhere in this book, it's very rare than any police officer gets convicted on criminal charges for a shooting death during a police action. The victory carried special significance since it came one year after the three detectives indicted for the 50-bullet shooting death of Sean Bell and wounding of his two friends had been acquitted in another judge-only trial. (Federal authorities are continuing to investigate the Bell case to determine whether any Federal criminal civil rights statutes were violated.)

On the day Lora's conviction was announced, many of Arzu's family members were in the courtroom, including his daughter Katherine and son Jeyson. "I'm happy that he was convicted," 24-year-old Katherine told the press. "He left me and my brother alone, without a father." With so many people prepared to rationalize any loss of life at the hands of the police, this point could never be emphasized too much.

"Let this verdict send a message to police officers all over this country," I added, "that if you recklessly kill, you will be held accountable."

Two months later, Clancy sentenced the officer to a one-to-three year prison term, acknowledging that he had "no criminal intent," but that he had nonetheless "incomprehensibly fired his gun five times."

I believe that these tragic shootings on the part of police will only stop occurring when the penalty for a police officer recklessly killing someone is jail time—as it was in this case. The penalty has to be steep enough to make police think twice before firing their revolvers.

Meanwhile, our civil case is moving forward. The fight continues.

INDEX

Abdur-Rashid, Imam Al-Hajj Talib, 123

Air France, 126, 132

Aleman, Rolando, 53, 56, 67

Alleyne, Vesean, 19–20, 22, 25–26

Amsterdam News, 136

Amy Ruth's restaurant, 96

Antoine, Patrick, 51

Arafat, Yassir, *xi*

Arzu, Fermin, 161–163

Arzu, Jeyson, 163

Arzu, Katherine, 163

Associated Press, 122–123, 136, 160

Baez, Anthony, 50

Barrios, Ruben, 85

Bell, Nicole Paultre, 9

Bell, Sean, 9–11, 70, 161, 163

Bellomo, Michael, 51, 54, 64

Benefield, Trent, 10

Bloomberg, Michael, 1, 5, 106–107, 116, 160

Brenner, Marie, 44–45

Bronx District Attorney's Office, 159, 162

Brooklyn Daily Eagle, 136

Brooklyn District Attorney's Office, 13, 47, 49, 51

Brown, Tracy, 23

Brown v. Board of Education, 2

Browne, Paul J., 152

Bruder, Thomas, 38–39. 52–54, 64–68

Bruno, Joseph, 24

Burkina Faso, 100, 121–123, 125–133, 141–143, 149, 151

Burkina Faso Association, 141

Bush, George W., 77, 92–95

Cable News Network (CNN), 106, 136, 138

Camile, Jacques, 29

Camp Garcia, 80

Cape Coast Castle, 134–135

Carrion, Adolfo, 80, 83, 91, 93–94, 96

Carter, Zachary, 45, 49–51, 61

Castro, Fidel, 106

CBS-TV, 118–119

Center for Constitutional Rights, 44

Chelsea Mini-Storage, 100, 104–105, 137, 152

Christian Solidarity International, 74, 76, 78

Clancy, Margaret, 162–163

Clinton, Bill, 43

Clinton, Hillary, 87

Club Rendez-Vous, 58, 62

Cochran, Johnnie, 23, 39–41, 44, 48, 52, 68, 100, 110, 150

Cohen, Dr. Joseph, 117–119

Compas, Dr. Jean Claude, 28

Connor, Bull, 97

Conroy, Bryan, 99, 101–103, 105, 113–115, 118–120, 138–139, 142–148, 152

Conyers, John, 44–45

Cuba, 105–107

Cuomo, Mario, 95

Davis, Cynthia, 94
Dewan, Shaila, 138, 140–141
Diallo, Amadou, *x*, 42, 55, 106, 108,
    116–117, 121, 123, 139, 143
Dinkins, David, 87, 96
Dixon, Monique, 20, 22–25
Dorismond, Patrick, 75
Dunleavy, Steve, 103–104
Durastanti, Armand, 145

Federal Bureau of Investigation
    (FBI), 50–52
Federal Metropolitan Detention
    Center, 86, 97
Ferrer, Fernando, 87, 95
Figeroux, Brian, 28–30, 32, 34
Fox television station, 136
Francisco's Funeraria, 122
Fulbright Jaworski law firm, 33
Fuste, José, 83

Ghana, 134–135
Ghandi, Mahatma, 94
Ginsburg, Nancy, 160
Ginsburg, William, 46
Giuliani, Rudolph (Rudy), 28, 30,
    37–38, 45, 80, 106, 151
George, Robert, 77
Goodman, Lieutenant Robert, 134
Graham, Reverend Billy, 77
Graham, Reverend Franklin, 77
Green, Esmin Elizabeth, 154–158
Green, Mark, 95
Guzman, Joseph, 9–10, 70–71

Haitian-American Alliance, 33
Hannity & Colmes, 90
Hardy, Michael, 9–10, 101, 103, 108,
    111–112, 115, 120, 149, 162
Harris, Eddie, 85
Harrison, Tecia, 155
Hess, Michael, 68

Hevesi, Alan, 95
Hynes, Charles, 49–51, 158

Jackson, Jacqueline, 95
Jackson, Reverend Jesse, 87–90, 134
Jacobs, Al, 11
Jacobs, Bill, 11, 33
Jacobs, Paul, 33
Johnson, Robert, 159, 162
Johnson, Sterling, 68

Kelly, Ray, 10, 106, 116, 139–141, 143
Kennedy, Robert, Jr., 91, 95
King, Coretta Scott, 94
King, Larry, *x–xi,* 33
King, Reverend Martin Luther, Jr., *x,*
    83, 90, 97, 131, 134
King, Rodney, *x*
King's County Hospital Center,
    154–158
Konate, Imam Souleimane, 123
Koppel, Ted, 46–47
Kornberg, Marvyn, 47, 52–53, 57–61

Legal Aid Society, 160
Levinson, Stanley, 131
Lewinsky, Monica, 46
Livotti, Francis, 50
London, Bernie, 149–151
London, Stuart, 145–146
Lora, Rafael, 161–163
Louima, Abner, *x,* 6, 27–28, 30–39,
    44–48, 50–53, 56–72, 89,
    111–112, 119, 150
    March for Justice for, *xi,* 33–37, 87
Louima, Micheline, 31, 46
Louima, Samantha, 32, 34, 56, 133

Mandela, Nelson, 94
Manhattan District Attorney's
    Office, 110–111, 115, 120, 122,
    138, 140

Manhattan Federal Courthouse, 149
Masjid Aqsa Mosque, 123
Medgar Evers College, 44
Meeks, Gregory, 96
Mollen, Milton, 45
Morgenthau, Robert, 115, 135, 140
MSNBC television station, 136
Muhammad, Akbar, 134

National Action Network, 7, 10, 33,
    37, 103, 108, 111, 113–114, 117,
    123, 137
NBC-TV, 118, 120
Neufeld, Peter, 39, 52, 68
New York 1 television station, 88, 119
New York City Department of
    Corrections, 158, 160
New York City Department of
    Investigation, 156–158
New York City Health and Hospitals
    Corporation (HHC), 155–157
New York Civil Liberties Union, 155
New York Daily News, 14, 21, 28,
    71–72, 89–90, 119, 136–137
New York Police Department
    (NYPD), 6, 10–11, 18, 29,
    38, 55, 60, 65, 99, 101, 103,
    105–106, 116–118, 120–121,
    125, 147, 152, 161–162
    Department of Internal Affairs,
    60, 118
    Staten Island Task Force, 105
New York Post, 7, 22, 77, 103, 136,
    139
New York State Mental Hygiene
    Legal Service, 155
New York Times, 25, 39, 47, 49,
    52, 91–92, 100, 116, 136, 138,
    140–141, 143–144, 152, 160, 162
Newsday, 136, 138
Nicholas, Jay, 58
Nickerson, Eugene, 52, 54–55, 57,

61–64, 66–67
Nicolas, Pastor Philius, 28, 30
Nicolas, Sam, 27–28, 63
Nightline, 46–47
Ninety-second Street Y, 105
Noerdlinger, Rachel, 85, 94

Obama, Barack, 44
Ogletree, Charles, 93

Pataki, George, 23–25, 80, 109,
    114–115
Pillersdorf, Gary, 16
Police Benevolent Association, 6,
    67–70
Pollak, Cheryl, 68
Powell, Colin, 77

Ramirez, Roberto, 80, 83, 91, 93–94
Rangel, Charlie, 87, 96
Reyes, Angel, 20–22, 25–26
Reyes, Diana, 20–21, 23–25
Rikers Island jail, 158–160
Robert N. Davoren Center, 159–160
Rivera, Dennis, 91, 95
Rivera, Jose, 80, 83, 91, 93–94
Robinson, Charnel, 159–160
Robinson, Christopher, 158–160
Rosario, Francisco, 53, 56, 67
Rynecki, Scott, 31, 140, 149

Safir, Howard, 38
St. Vincent's Hospital, 104–105, 118
Sampson, Reverend Albert (Al), *xii*,
    134
Sanfo, Salimata, 102, 126–127, 133,
    135–143, 146, 148–149, 151
Scheck, Barry, 39, 68
Schoer, Michael, 61
Schofield, Mark, 60
Schumer, Charles (Chuck), 87
Schwarz, Charles, 39, 47, 53–54,

64–68
September 11, 2001 terrorist attacks, 4
Sharpton, Ashley, 87–88
Sharpton, Dominique, 87–88
Sharpton, Kathy, 87–88
Sharpton, Reverend Al, *ix-xiii*, 6, 33–36, 41–43, 73–97, 107–108, 111–116, 121, 124, 133–135, 137–138, 140–141
    2004 presidential campaign, 80–81, 133–134
    and the New Jersey Four, 41–43
    imprisonment for trespass on Vieques, *xi*, 6, 79–97
    modern-day slavery fact-finding trip to Sudan, 73–79
    peace delegation to Ghana, *xii*, 134
Shepard, Andrea, 103
Shepard, Shirley, 103
Silver, Sheldon, 23–24
Spruill, Alberta, 106, 110, 116
Stansbury, Timothy, 143–144, 146
Staten Island Ferry crash, 18–19
Straus, Robert H., 146–148
Sudan, *xi*, 73–80
    civil war, 73–74, 78
    Darfur region of, 74
    modern-day slave trade in, *xi*, 73–79
Sudanese People's Liberation Army, 73–74
Summers, Lawrence, 134

Telemondo television station, 117
The View, 46
Thomas, Carl, 28–30, 32, 34
Thompson, Kenneth, 58
Towns, Edolphus (Ed), 32, 34, 133, 141
Turetzky, Eric, 56, 60

U.S. Attorney's Office, Eastern District of New York, 45, 49–50, 61
U.S. Justice Department, 42, 155–156, 158
U.S. Navy, *xi*, 6, 73, 79–80, 82–83, 91–93, 95
    bombing of Vieques, *xi*, 6, 73, 79–80, 82–83, 91–93, 95
    civil disobedience against, 79–80, 91
    prosecutors deputized as U.S. attorneys, 82–83
U.S. State Department, 132–133
U.S. Treasury Department, 105

Vallone, Peter, 95
Vanity Fair magazine, 44
Vesean's Law, 19, 24–25
Vieques, Island of, *xi*, 73, 79–85, 91–97
Village Voice, 159
Volpe, Justin, 30, 38, 47, 50–67
Volpe, Robert, 55–56, 59

Walters, Barbara, 45–46
Warwick, Kenneth, 60–61
Weissenstein, Michael, 122
West, Dr. Cornel, *xii*, 134
Whitman, Christie, 41–42
Wiese, Thomas, 39, 52–54, 64–68
WINS radio station, 117
Wirta, John, 20, 22–23, 25–26
WWOR-TV (Channel 9), 117–118

Zongo, Adama Somkeita, 100, 111–112, 125, 149
Zongo, Daouda, 133, 135–143, 149, 151
Zongo, Ousmane, 6–7, 99–102, 104–133, 135, 137–144, 147–149, 151–152